COMPLETE**FINGERSTYLE**
BASSTECHNIQUE

The Complete Guide to Mastering Essential Modern Bass Fingerstyle Technique

DAN**HAWKINS**

FUNDAMENTAL**CHANGES**

Complete Fingerstyle Bass Technique

The Complete Guide to Mastering Essential Modern Bass Fingerstyle Technique

ISBN: 978-1-78933-238-4

Published by **www.fundamental-changes.com**

www.fundamental-changes.com

Over 13,000 fans on Facebook: **FundamentalChangesInGuitar**

Instagram: **FundamentalChanges**

For over 350 Free Guitar Lessons with Videos Check Out

www.fundamental-changes.com

Cover Image Copyright: Shutterstock – Miha Travnik

Contents

Introduction

The most common question I get asked by new bass students is "What do I need to learn first?" It's a difficult question to answer because there are many elements that combine to create an excellent musician. These include understanding rhythm, playing in time, applying music theory and, of course, learning loads of basslines to develop your musical feel.

But there is one element without which all of the above will be difficult to achieve: *technique*. Invariably, I tell students to focus on technique first, because quite simply it is the means by which you express any musical idea. Once you're able to control your bass and play with ease, you can concentrate solely on making music.

First, this book will teach you the key techniques you need in order to control your bass, play in time, build solid grooves and avoid any pains or strains. Along the way I'll give you plenty of tips on how to build successful practice habits, set goals, and develop your musicianship.

Next, we'll work on refining your technique with more challenging ideas such as raking, executing smooth position shifts, string skipping and more. All aspects of fingerstyle bass are covered and each technique is built into a musical example you can use in your playing right away. Playing great music, after all, is the end result of all this technical study.

When building technique, it's important that you take your time and go at your own pace. Learning well is more important than learning quickly. We are laying a foundation here that will serve your bass playing for years to come, whatever style of music you're passionate about. You wouldn't want to buy a house built on faulty foundations, so treat your bass technique the same way! Play the exercises in this book until they are firmly under your fingers to ensure you have mastered each one.

Have fun and enjoy mastering your bass!

Dan.

Building Good Habits

In his book *The Talent Code*, author Dan Coyle discusses myelin – a substance in the brain that helps electrical impulses to flow more efficiently. The more you repeat an action, the more myelin is formed, allowing you to perform the action more quickly next time. This means that your practice habits are extremely important. If you work slowly and build good habits, your brain will reinforce them for you. The flip side of this is that it takes some hard work to overwrite bad habits once they've been formed, so start right and continue to reinforce the good habits you'll learn here.

When you're learning something new on bass, follow this process to ensure you're building the desirable *muscle memory:*

- Follow the instructions closely

- Play slowly and cleanly. Listen carefully for unwanted noise and work to eliminate it

- Make sure BOTH hands are working the way you want them to. This will differ between exercises, but as a general rule you should aim to minimise excess movement, watch out for muscle strain, and control unwanted string noise

- Build speed in small increments once you're comfortable with the previous steps

If you can cultivate the patience needed to develop these good habits, you will nurture those useful myelin connections in your brain. Persevere, because this process does take time, dedication and effort.

Practice

There's a lot to absorb on your musical journey, so it's important to be selective and focus on what really matters. It's easy to just sit and noodle on your bass, rather than practicing in a purposeful manner, so here I'll share my tips for keeping your practice sessions sharp and productive. These principles will help you to get the most out of this book.

Be consistent

Practicing for ten minutes every day is better than an hour once a week. Building muscle memory comes from repetition and is the result of regular practice. Using a practice journal can really help to clarify your goals and track your progress. If you're struggling to find time to work on your bass playing, do an honest audit of how you spend your free time. If you *really* want to improve then you can swap some Netflix/social media/gaming time for practice.

Make it easy to practice

Keep your bass on a stand so it's always close to hand and keep your practice space distraction-free. It constantly amazes me how simple and effective this tip is. When you get to your instrument you should be ready to go without having to find your laptop, music stand, strap, pedals and so on. Create an environment that you love going into – one that is distraction free and inspires you to play.

Relax

This can be easier said than done, but relaxing your mind and body makes playing easier and helps to avoid injuries. Pay attention to the level of tension in your whole body as you play. About once a year, I play multiplayer Halo on Xbox with a group of friends. I feel pressure to maintain my status as "Halo Champ" (my friends aren't great to be fair!) and this pressure results in high levels of tension in my hands without me knowing. About an hour in, I'm completely out of action and in severe pain. I've seen many bass players use the "Halo Hand" approach and it's not good for the wrists/fingers (or the music). When you are tense, your breathing tends to change and this can affect performance. Focus on relaxing your hands, wrists and shoulders while breathing normally.

Plan your practice

No matter how long or short your practice session is, get the most out of it by having a clear plan. Divide your time into specific slots to get a well-rounded, focused practice session. Warm up with some technical exercises (see my book *Creative Bass Technique Exercises*), then divide your remaining time between specific things you need to work on. This routine can be completely tailored to your goals and will make a few hours of practice fly by.

Address your weaknesses

Be honest with yourself about your playing and don't shy away from working on your weaknesses. This can be tough because it will test your patience and perseverance. Most people want to hear themselves playing something that sounds great already, but absolutely no improvement comes from that. Progress stems from working on the things you *can't* do. Remember that if something is difficult, it may just be unfamiliar. You will only get better at it by working on it and building familiarity.

Practice with a metronome

Use a metronome, drum machine, drum loops or, even better, play with a great drummer. Your sense of groove and time is perhaps the most important skill you can develop as a musician. Prioritise this above all else.

Break things down

Being a good bassist and having excellent technique is about getting hundreds of tiny things working well at the same time. When isolated, these things aren't too difficult – the trick is putting them all together flawlessly. That's why you practice. When you're learning something new and things don't seem to be going smoothly, slow it down and dissect the exercise. Try practicing the right hand by itself or learning the notes without the rhythm. As you get more experienced, you will get better at identifying and isolating the challenges.

If you want to play fast, start slow!

This is one of the big themes of this book and the best approach to developing good technique. Your brain needs to consolidate the complex relationship between your hands and the instrument. Muscle memory is the process by which you learn to do anything automatically, and the best way to develop it is by playing slowly and building speed gradually over time.

Avoid pain

As you work through this book, it's important that you're aware of any discomfort in your body and do not play through a certain type of pain.

There are two types of pain:

The first is discomfort due to skin abrasion which might result in blisters. This is normal. The more you play, the more stress you are placing on your fingertips. The body's response to this is to build more layers of skin without nerve endings, called calluses. These take time to form. This pain should only occur during the first few weeks and is nothing to worry about.

The second type is joint or muscle pain. This is the type you need to be mindful of.

If you feel any kind of muscular or joint pain, then stop practicing for the day. Ensure you're relaxed when you play and that your hands are in the correct position. Playing through muscular discomfort can lead to problems like carpel tunnel syndrome or repetitive strain injury. If you continue to experience joint or muscle pain, you should see a specialist.

Parts of The Bass

Before we begin our journey, it's important to know what each part of your bass is called. I'll refer to these names throughout the book. If you forget or get confused, you can always flip back and look at the diagram below.

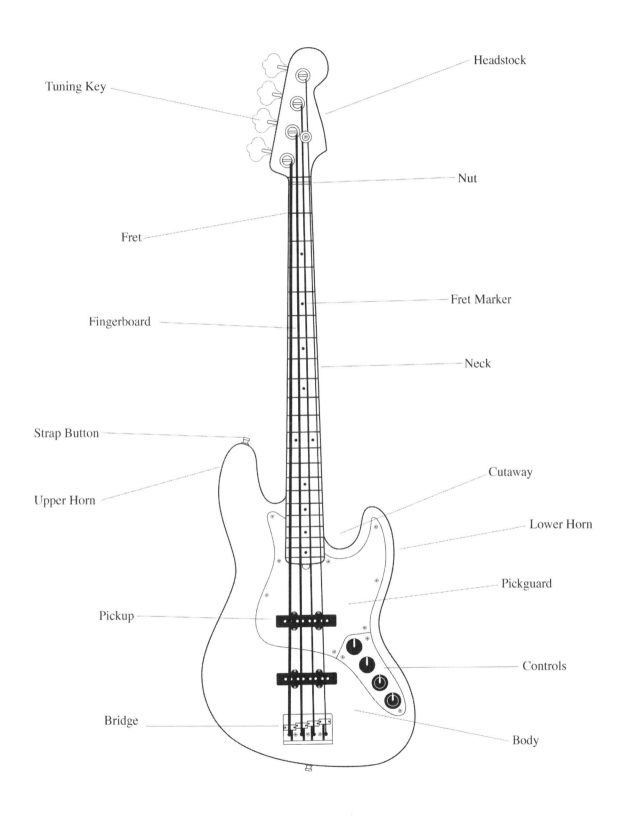

Get the Audio

The audio files for this book are available to download for free from **www.fundamental-changes.com.** The link is in the top right-hand corner. Click on the "Guitar" link then simply select this book title from the drop-down menu and follow the instructions to get the audio.

We recommend that you download the files directly to your computer, not to your tablet, and extract them there before adding them to your media library. You can then put them onto your tablet, iPod or burn them to CD. On the download page there are instructions and we also provide technical support via the contact form.

For over 350 free guitar lessons with videos check out:

www.fundamental-changes.com

Over 13,000 fans on Facebook: **FundamentalChangesInGuitar**

Tag us for a share on Instagram: **FundamentalChanges**

Fundamental Techniques

As this book progresses, the challenge of each exercise increases gradually. If you already have the basics down, you may want to skip forward a few pages. However, the first lessons are all about building strong foundations, so I do advise you start from the beginning – it's always good to refresh the basics.

This section of the book focuses on the components that combine to form good technique. Getting these elements right is the key to becoming a great bass player.

Holding the Bass When Sitting

Finding a comfortable seating position with the bass can make practice more enjoyable, reduce injury, and help you progress more quickly.

If you're sitting down, the bass should come into contact with three parts of your body:

1. The curve of the bottom of the bass sits on your thigh.

2. The upper horn rests against the front of your ribcage/chest

3. Your plucking hand forearm rests on the body of the bass above the bridge

These three points of contact keep the bass steady, allowing your fretting hand to move freely.

A common mistake is to support the weight of the neck with the fretting hand. When you take your fretting hand off the neck, the instrument shouldn't move.

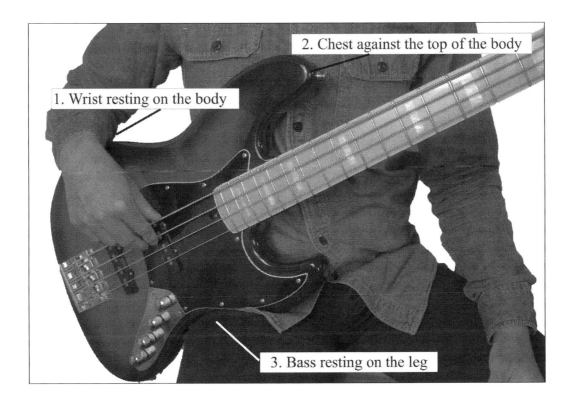

Angle the neck of your bass slightly upward (see above) and slightly away from you (see below). Holding the bass this way gives your fretting hand complete access to the full range of the neck.

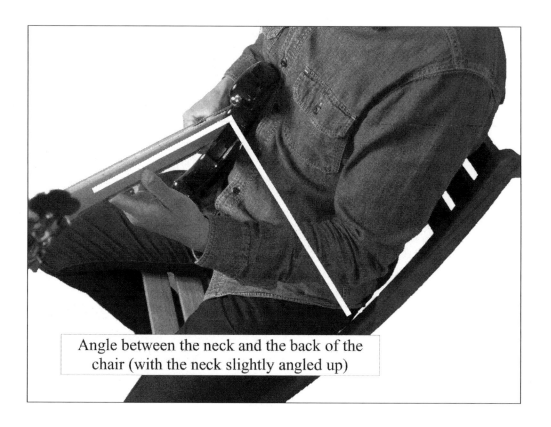

Angle between the neck and the back of the chair (with the neck slightly angled up)

Take your time getting comfortable with this position. If your bass has an irregular shape or weight distribution, you may need to use a strap to keep it supported or experiment with a classical style posture. The classical position, used by classical guitarists, involves resting the bass on the left leg, angling the neck at 45 degrees above the horizon, and may require the use of a foot stool.

When standing, I recommend you set your strap so that the bass is in the same position as when seated. This means that your playing position will be consistent between practice and performance.

Now you're ready to start making some sound.

The Plucking Hand

The plucking hand is responsible for picking each note. There are a variety of plucking hand techniques, patterns and placements you will need to become familiar with, but we'll start with the basics.

Anchoring

Anchoring helps to stabilize your plucking hand and stop unwanted strings from ringing. Rest the thumb of the plucking hand on the top of the pickup (see image on the next page), so that it is anchored to the instrument and not floating. Many players keep the thumb anchored on the pickup at all times, however, when playing the higher strings, you can anchor on the low E or A strings to stop them from ringing accidentally. Now that the hands in place, let's look at making some sound.

Alternate plucking

Alternate plucking is the most common way to pick the strings and involves alternating the index (*i*) and middle (*m*) fingers. The goal is to develop an even sound and control over both fingers.

Example 1a involves alternate plucking on each string. Anchor your thumb on the pickup throughout and alternate pluck each *open string* four times. (Open strings are indicated by a "0" in the tab and show that no note is fretted).

Keep your index and middle fingers slightly curled and pluck using your fingertips. The two fingers should be close together or even brushing against each other as you pluck upwards towards the thumb.

You might notice the lower strings continue to ring out, or start to ring, while you are playing the higher strings. Moving the anchor to the E or A string will help to combat this. Once (and only once) you are comfortable with keeping your thumb on the pickup throughout, try moving the anchor to the E (4th) string as you change to the higher strings.

Example 1a

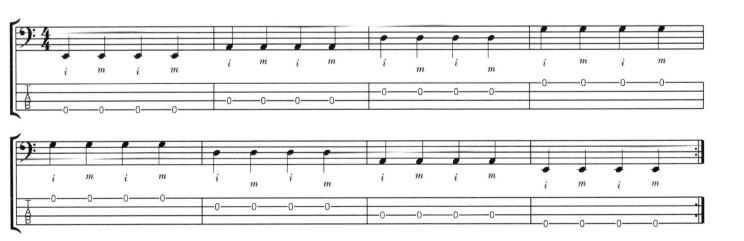

Rest Strokes

The rest stroke is a fundamental technique where you pluck a string then come to rest on the underside of the string below.

Note that whenever we refer to "up", "down", "higher", "lower", "above" or "below", we are talking about *pitch*. The string *below* the A (3rd) string is the E (4th) string, as it is the next string that is lower in pitch (despite the plucking action being a physical movement upwards towards your head!) Also note that the words "stroke" and "pluck" are used interchangeably throughout this text.

Rest strokes will be used on every string except the E (4th) string, which has no string below to rest on. Rest strokes have a few useful benefits, including muting the lower string and allowing us to play faster and harder.

The image below shows the position your index finger will come to rest in after plucking the A string. Notice how the finger is now in the perfect position to pluck the low E string.

Use Example 1b to develop your rest stroke technique. Anchor the thumb on the pickup, pluck the A string, and let the finger follow through to rest on the E string. Keep this pattern going for every stroke. Repeat this movement on the D string in bars three and four.

Practice this exercise until each note has an even volume and sound. Pay close attention to the rhythm and make sure the 1/8th notes (the shorter notes on beats two and three) are evenly dividing the beat. Listen to the audio example to hear exactly how it should sound.

Example 1b

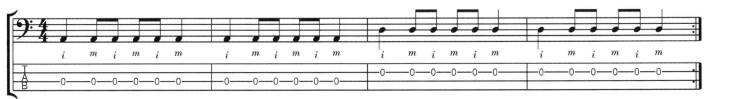

Changing Strings

Changing strings can be a little bit tricky. A single bassline can contain multiple string changes and skips and it's our job to be able to execute those lines without losing the flow and groove. Luckily, there is a simple rule that applies to almost all basslines: use alternate plucking when changing strings *except* when moving from one string to the string directly below.

When changing from one string to the next lowest string you will use a technique called *raking*. Raking helps us change strings smoothly and efficiently. I'll cover more advanced raking in the next chapter but it's essential to get the basics down now.

Raking is where you pluck two strings in a row using the *same* finger instead of alternating your middle and index. It's the natural evolution of the rest stroke that we just learnt.

As you know, when playing rest strokes, your finger comes to rest on the string below. If the next note you need to play is on the string you're resting on, then it makes sense to reuse the finger that's already on it. This makes string changing a lot less awkward.

In Example 1c, pluck the G (1st) string with your index finger, then continue all the way to the E string. Repeat the same thing using your middle finger. Focus on your timing and make each note last the exact same length. Don't worry about the strings ringing out for now, we'll tackle muting in the next section.

Now try alternate plucking and feel the difference. You'll find it's much easier to use raking.

Example 1c

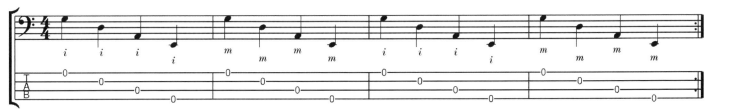

Example 1d is a real-world example of raking. It features an *alternating bassline,* which just means that the bassline alternates between two notes. The first two bars require raking with the index finger and bars three and four require raking with the middle finger. Watch out for three string rakes on the last beat of bars two and four.

Example 1d

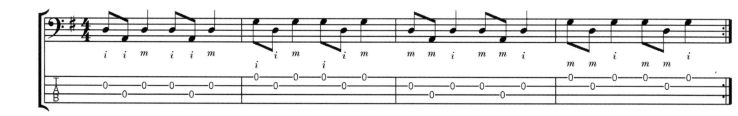

Muting

Muting techniques are essential for controlling unwanted string noise and note length. As you saw in the last two examples, strings will continue to ring over each other unless we mute them. In this section you'll learn two important ways of muting with the plucking hand that will keep your playing clean. We'll discuss fretting hand muting in the next section.

Example 1e involves muting a string with the plucking-hand fingers. Pluck using alternate strokes then cut off the final note on beat four by lightly resting the next plucking finger in the sequence on the string. This finger is then used to play the following note. In other words, in bar one you will play the last note with the index finger then mute it with the middle finger. The first note of bar two will then be played with the middle finger, and so on.

To master this technique, try playing the exercise in time with the drumbeat on the backing track. Listen to the audio example and pay attention to how long I let the note ring before I mute it. It can be tempting to cut it off early, so be sure to give it a full beat's length. Remember, the ending of a note is just as important to the groove as its beginning.

Example 1e

The second method involves muting with the anchor. To mute the open E string on beat 4 of bar one, move your anchor from the pickup onto the string. Again, make sure this movement happens at the exact moment you want the note to stop. You also need to mute the D string in bars two and four on the final beat with the middle finger of your plucking hand.

Example 1f

These exercises should demonstrate how important controlling the length of notes is to the groove and feel of a bassline. We will learn more muting techniques as we progress through the book and, through practice, you'll learn the benefits of each one and your personal preferences.

The Fretting Hand Position

Now that we know how to both set a string in motion and stop it, we can start to look at the *fretting hand*. The fretting hand's job is to hold down notes and "shorten" the length of a string by connecting it with a fret (the steel wires running along the fretboard). This change in length results in a change of pitch.

In this section you'll learn how to place your fretting hand correctly on the neck to give you maximum dexterity and freedom.

Start by placing the thumb gently on the back of the neck behind the fifth fret. Ensure it is about halfway up the neck. This halfway height means that the thumb isn't hooked over the top or sliding off the bottom – it's in the middle, so the fingers are supported and can easily apply pressure to the strings.

Slowly bring your fingers to rest on the G string. Keep your fingers relaxed and slightly curved. There is no need to spread or stretch them apart, just find a comfortable natural placement. Lastly, line up your thumb directly behind your middle finger. It should resemble the image below.

Keep your thumb in position and move your fingers to rest on the D string. Now rest them all on the A string, and finally the E string.

The image below demonstrates a very important fretting technique called *one finger per fret*. The fingers are spaced out so that they each line up with their own fret. Now repeat the previous placement exercise using the one-finger-per-fret spacing. You may need to start higher up the neck where the fret spacing is narrower. Try it around the 12th fret.

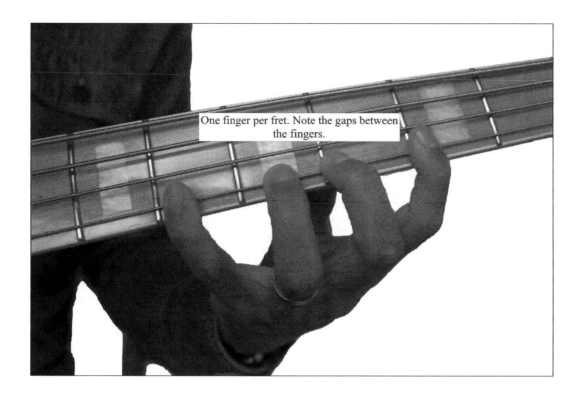

One finger per fret. Note the gaps between the fingers.

To fret a note, place your finger on the string *just behind* the fret and press down with your fingertip. If you hear any buzzing, you may need to press harder or move closer to the fret. Adjust the position of your finger until a buzz-free tone is produced.

Now let's take a look at using all four fretting-hand fingers with a few technical exercises.

Combining Hands

The following exercises will develop fretting hand strength as well as the coordination between both hands.

This first exercise starts at the fifth fret with a one-finger-per-fret approach. Use alternate plucking and pay attention to the fretting hand fingerings indicated below each note.

Even though the frets are slightly closer here than at the first fret, you may still struggle with this stretch. If you can't make the stretch, you can let the fingers relax and huddle around the finger that's doing the fretting. This will make the exercise more manageable, just make sure that you still follow the correct fingering.

Example 1g

The next step is to use some different patterns for the fretting hand. As you gain familiarity with this exercise, work to develop your stretch and reduce finger huddling. It may take some time to develop, so don't be disheartened. Example 1g shows the 1-4-3-2 pattern.

Example 1h

To keep things varied and to prepare you for whatever licks life may throw at you, you should work through all possible fretting combinations for the four fingers. Here are all the different permutations you can practice. I suggest picking 4 or 5 of these each day to use as a warm-up, practicing each one for 30 seconds with a metronome.

1-2-3-4	2-1-3-4	3-1-2-4	4-1-2-3
1-2-4-3	2-1-4-3	3-1-4-2	4-1-3-2
1-3-2-4	2-3-1-4	3-2-1-4	4-2-1-3
1-3-4-2	2-3-4-1	3-2-4-1	4-2-3-1
1-4-2-3	2-4-1-3	3-4-1-2	4-3-1-2
1-4-3-2	2-4-3-1	3-4-2-1	4-3-2-1

One Finger in The Future

Now that you understand the basics of fretting and plucking, we can look at some concepts that will help to refine your technique. These will help you to play smoother, faster and more easily.

The first of these concepts is the *one finger in the future* technique. It's the key to developing smooth-sounding, effortless technique by anticipating what's coming next. For example, if you're fretting a note with your first finger and the next note is to be played with the fourth finger on the string below, the fourth finger should be ready and waiting over that note.

Here's a great exercise to practice this concept for the fretting hand. Start by hovering your fingers over a four-fret span. Every time your pinkie finger is fretting a note, move the index finger up in anticipation of the next note. I suggest practicing this freely and out of time at first, as the coordination might take some practice, but before you know it, you'll be moving up and down the neck like a graceful caterpillar.

Example 1i

Now let's apply the *one finger in the future* principle to the plucking hand. When making the ascending string changes in bars 5-8, move your next plucking finger into position ready to pluck the new string as soon as you've played the last note of the previous string. You can do this either by planting it on the string early, or simply hovering over the string.

NB: the descending string changes in bars 1-4 will use raking.

Example 1j

This next exercise combines the previous two techniques and makes for a great warm-up and technique builder. When going from beat 4 in bar four to beat 1 in bar five, use the first anticipation method. Sneak the index finger over fret 6 while the pinky is still holding fret 8. Then plant your plucking fingers as early as possible on the ascending string changes in bars 5-8.

When you repeat the exercise, you can choose to keep moving up one fret at a time or shift back to the starting fret. Either way, make sure your first finger is in place early.

Practice this exercise across the whole range of your instrument. It will help you familiarise yourself with the entire fretboard.

Example 1k

To recap, you can create a lot of variations based around these fretting-hand exercises and I encourage you to do so. Make them a part of your daily practice routine and you'll build your technique in no time. As little as ten minutes a day will yield very positive results and you'll know you're getting better because it will feel easier and sound good.

Make sure to pay attention to the following:

FRETTING HAND	PLUCKING HAND
Thumb behind the neck (roughly behind middle finger)	Thumb anchored
Gaps between fingers	Alternating fingers
One finger per fret	Rest strokes
Fingers slightly curled and not collapsing	Fingers slightly curled
Wrist as straight as possible	Only pluck as hard as you need to
Only press as hard as you need to	Choose where to pluck for the tone you want.

Fretting-Hand Muting

The fretting hand also shares some of the responsibility for muting, and practicing this technique will have a profound effect on your bass playing.

Example 1l demonstrates two crucial fretting hand muting techniques.

To stop the open E string in bar one, lightly touch your fretting hand fingers against the string. The key is to use a gentle patting motion, light enough so that no unwanted notes sound or fret noise is generated.

To stop the F# note in bar three, gently release pressure on the fretted note while still remaining in contact with the string. You can think of this as a *half-release*. This requires developing control over how much pressure you're applying and will take some practice. You can stop any fretted note this way.

It's also common to combine both techniques by half-releasing a fretted note *and* patting down any fingers higher than the fretting finger.

Example 11 has a backing track to play along to. Listen to the recorded example and pay attention to the timing of the muting. See if you can get the same rhythmic accuracy from both muting techniques.

Example 11

Advanced Muting Techniques

So far, we've looked at a couple of basic muting techniques for each hand. In this section we will explore more advanced muting techniques. These will allow us to play more challenging basslines and exercises with precision and clarity. Having a wealth of muting techniques at your disposal will keep you prepared for any situation and never leave you frustrated wondering why you can't get a bassline to sound like the record.

Floating Thumb

The *floating thumb* technique involves straightening out your thumb and allowing it to rest against the strings you're not playing. Although we give up the benefits of our anchor, we gain a highly versatile mute. This is useful when playing notes on the D and G strings or when you have a line with lots of string changing. As illustrated in the image below, the floating thumb can mute the lower three strings and is also free to glide during rapid string changes.

Example 1m shows a real-world application of the floating thumb technique. It requires you to transition from an anchored thumb in bars one and three to a floating thumb in bars two and four. Use your fretting hand to keep the open E note short and use the time in the rests to transition your thumb between positions.

Example 1m

Ring Finger

The ring finger of the plucking hand can also be used to mute strings as seen in the image below. This technique, along with the floating thumb, are especially useful for extended-range bass playing. Extended-range basses have 5 strings or more and require more advanced muting as a result.

In Example 1n, after playing the E string, mute it by planting your ring finger on it as you proceed to pluck the higher strings.

Example 1n

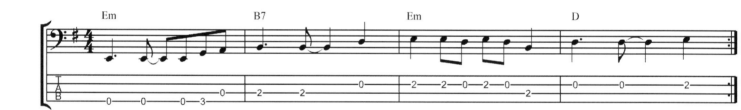

Fretting Fingers

The final advanced muting technique involves some clever tweaks to your fretting hand fingers to keep things quiet. Remember, muting doesn't just mean silencing a string you've played, it also means keeping the strings you're not playing from ringing.

Example 1o is a bassline built around octaves. Each bar contains only one note but played in a different register of the instrument. This is a very common shape which you'll come across a lot, so really take the time to get this under your fingers.

Start by using the first finger to fret the A string but don't use the very tip of the finger. Let the tip of the finger overhang so that it comes into contact with the underside of the E string. Then, the lower part of the finger gently rests on the D string. This is an extremely effective muting technique, all taken care of with one finger. It's also very useful for slap technique when the slap/pop hand is far too busy to do any muting.

Notice how the plucking pattern is not alternate – you could see this as a one-finger-per-string approach. All the notes on the A string are played with the index finger and all the notes on the G string are played with the longer middle finger. Also note that the use of the fourth finger to fret the octave (the higher note in each bar) is not in keeping with the one-finger-per-fret technique. This makes the stretch a lot more manageable. There's a funky hip-hop backing track to play this over.

Example 1o

You can use Example 1p to practice this muting technique. Whenever you fret a note on the low E string, ensure your finger is slightly touching the A string to make sure it's not going to sound. Whenever playing the A string, make sure your fretting finger is muting both the E and D strings.

I'm also breaking away from the one-finger-per-fret concept here because this area of the neck has a wider fret spacing. When you're playing around the 1st fret, you can use the little finger to play the 3rd fret to reduce the stretch and any strain on the hand.

Example 1p

Now that you have a wide range of muting techniques under your fingers, you can start to experiment and pick the most effective or comfortable one for each situation. It's completely normal to have one or two muting methods that you use more than others. As long as strings aren't unintentionally ringing out, it doesn't matter which technique (or combination of techniques) you use.

Lastly, it can be incredibly beneficial to record yourself playing these exercises. This allows you to listen back and analyse the integrity of your muting. You might pick up on things you missed in the moment that need to be addressed.

Advanced Techniques

As you learn more basslines, you'll come across riffs and licks that require some additional techniques. Each technique in this section has a specific benefit that is broken down in detail, so you will know when, why, and how to use it. This section is also a source of technical exercises that will help you to develop speed and dexterity.

Advanced Raking

We have already looked at basic raking technique, now let's explore some more challenging musical exercises that combine both hands to play more complicated rhythms. These exercises are more like what you would encounter when learning actual basslines.

Example 2a uses raking to pluck a 1/16th note figure across three strings. The index finger is indicated for the rake but also try it with the middle finger. This technique should feel like a natural evolution of the rest stroke. As you're playing what can feel like one continuous stroke, it's very common to lose track of the timing and rush. Practice playing along to the recording with me and lock it in.

Also, we aren't trying to play a chord, so time the release of your fretting hand fingers so that the notes don't ring out together. The open E string will also need to be muted by the fretting hand.

Example 2a

Raking works well when you're playing a passage that contains only one note on each string like the following example. Use the suggested fingering and rake with index or middle fingers.

Example 2b

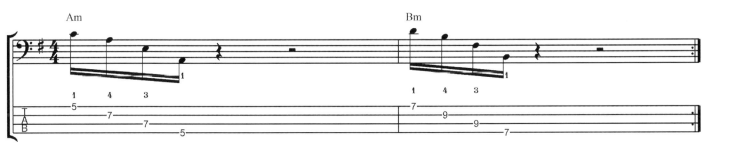

You can also rake across just two strings as in the following exercise that uses an A Minor Pentatonic lick. When used in conjunction with alternate plucking, this technique can lead to some very impressive playing. There is an alternate way to fret the raked section, which we'll discuss in the next example.

Example 2c

Rolling/Barring

In Example 2c the index and middle fingers both played notes on the second fret. However, it would have been more efficient to use one finger to roll across both strings. In Example 2d, instead of using the tip of the finger to fret the note on the G string, flatten the finger slightly so the string is now closer to the first crease on your finger. This moves the tip closer to the D string so you can now *roll* your fingertip onto fret 2 of the D string. Use these two notes and roll back and forth until this technique feels comfortable.

Example 2d

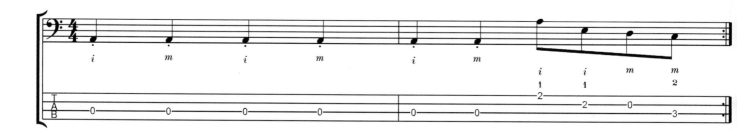

The following exercises will demonstrate *rolling* in a variety of musical contexts. Example 2e is a useful pattern that requires rolling with the ring finger. To get the finger into the correct position, keep it straighter than normal. The notes should sound separately and not overlap. There is a backing track you can use for this exercise.

Example 2e

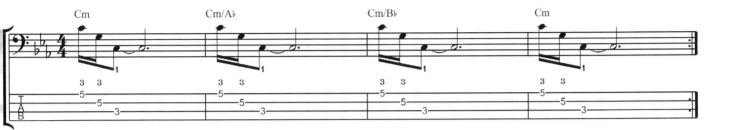

In Example 2f we are going to combine raking and rolling to play a fill using the minor pentatonic shape below. The root note is indicated by squares and the numbers show which fingers to use.

A Minor Pentatonic

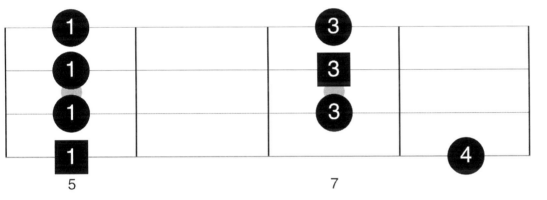

You can come up with your own phrases around this idea by changing direction, rhythm and tempo. Play this one slowly at first and notice when rolling and raking occur.

Example 2f

Example 2g shows how you might expect to see the previous example in a musical situation. It's exactly the same riff but played using 1/16th notes. Reaching this speed will take patience and consistent practice but is definitely achievable.

Example 2g

Here is a good strategy for increasing your speed. You can use Example 2g or anything you're working on that you want to be able to play faster.

Using a metronome, find what you consider a comfortable tempo for the exercise. Note that tempo, then notch it up by no more than 5BPM in your next practice session. If you hit a plateau and cannot increase the tempo comfortably, decrease it, returning to the tempo of the previous session and start the process again from there.

This approach ensures you are not trying to run before you can walk. It will help you make consistent progress by forcing you to really master every tempo before you can move on.

Hand Shifts

Hand shifting is the ability to smoothly and accurately move your fretting hand around the neck. As you change positions, the aim is to keep your thumb behind the neck and in constant contact with it. For added stability, your fretting hand fingers can also be touching the strings as you shift.

Let's keep things simple by playing a bassline on just one string. You're going to shift your hand position in each bar and fret all of the notes with your index finger. Follow the notation/TAB and use the rests to execute the shifts. Listen to the audio example for the rhythm and play along with the backing track when you're ready.

Example 2h

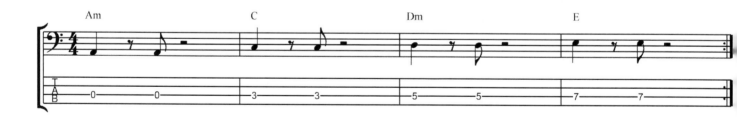

Example 2i adds a melodic line in bar four. Use one finger per fret for the last bar and shift back while you play the open A note on the repeat.

Example 2i

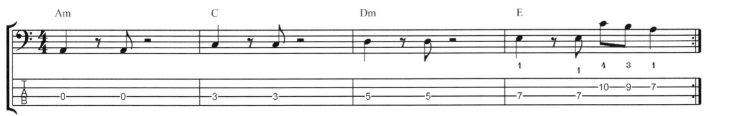

The aim of these exercises is to develop the ability to shift your hand position swiftly and accurately. Example 2j is a C Major scale on the A string which spans the range of the neck. Stick to the fingering suggestions and slide your thumb across the back of the neck to help you shift smoothly. Make sure you play the notes for their full length.

Example 2j

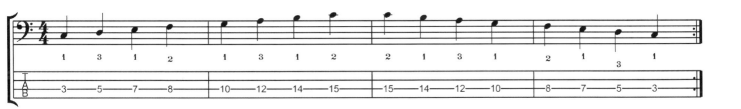

The following octave exercise will work on smooth shifting as well as a stretch in your fretting hand. Use your index finger to pluck the lower strings and the longer middle finger to pluck the octaves.

In this example you may prefer to use the pinkie finger for the octave. One finger per fret would mean using the third finger, which you can do if it's easier for you, but the fourth finger requires less of a stretch.

There's a jazz funk backing track for this one.

Example 2k

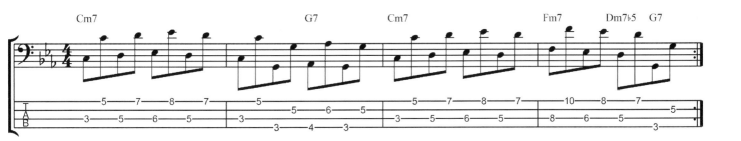

Thumb Pivot

If you only need to execute a small shift, an alternative option is a thumb pivot. Using the fretting hand thumb on the back of the neck, you can keep your hand in one position and pivot the thumb to quickly access a slightly higher register. This technique enables you to shift position without the fretting hand actually sliding anywhere.

Without playing anything, place your fretting hand on the neck as if you're about to play. Keep the thumb roughly behind the middle finger. The thumb tip should be pointing up towards the ceiling, as if you're giving a thumbs-up sign. Now twist your wrist so that the thumb points to the bass head and is parallel to the neck. Take a look where your fingers end up – higher up the neck! We can use this technique in our playing.

Follow the fingering on this "Duck" Dunn style RnB line. Use the thumb pivot to reach those higher notes and do it quickly, keeping contact between the thumb and neck. The rhythm is quite syncopated so listen to the audio example closely.

Example 2l

The next example is a similar idea but has a more complicated melody in the pivoted position. The goal here is to leave the thumb in the same spot throughout the whole example.

Example 2m

Pivoting and hand shifting can be used at the same time to help you get around more easily. We'll leave pivoting for now, but it'll make a reappearance in the Expressive Techniques section.

String Skipping

Example 2n introduces the concept of *string skipping*. Skipping over strings when you pluck presents interesting technical challenges for both hands. In the exercise below, notice how the plucking pattern starts with the middle finger. This means that the longer middle finger is also used to pluck the higher string. This makes the string skip a lot more manageable and can be the difference between playing in time or struggling to keep up. Listen to the audio then try the exercise.

Example 2n

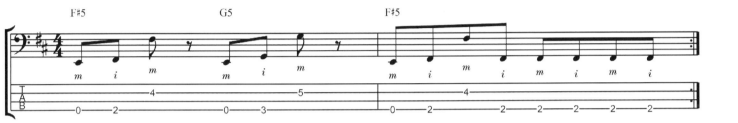

The next example is based around octaves. This time it makes sense to start plucking with the shorter index finger, leaving the middle ready to pluck the higher string. You can then use alternate plucking throughout. Pay attention to the hand shift going from the second to third bar. Since the patterns are the same throughout, you can keep your hand set in the same shape as you shift.

Example 2o

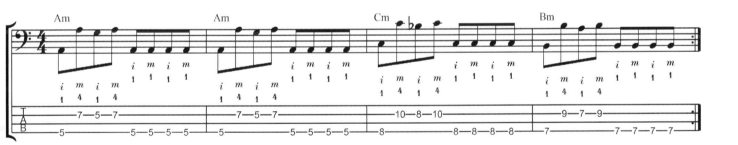

Let's look at an even bigger jump from the root note to a minor 10th (G# to B). Again, it's the index finger plucking the low string while the middle finger plucks the higher one. By always plucking the E string with your index finger, you free up the middle finger to pluck higher strings. You can either fret the first two notes with your index fingertip or you can use the rolling technique, playing the second note with a lower part of your finger (somewhere behind the knuckle).

Example 2p

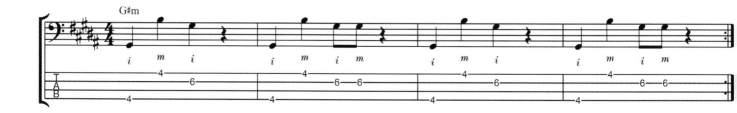

Example 2pii takes the same line, this time moving to a different chord. To get the transition sounding smooth you'll need to shift quickly from the 4th to the 9th fret. Take advantage of the quarter note rest to make the jump!

Example 2pii

Extended Fingering

Extended fingering is a way of stretching out of the four-fret span of the one-finger-per-fret system.

Before we get into it, first an explanation. When we refer to a fretting hand *position,* we are referring to the fret where the index finger is placed. For example, tenth position means you line up the index finger with fret 10. The remaining fingers span the next three frets using the one-finger-per-fret rule.

Extended fingering is where the index or pinkie finger stretches out of that position to play more notes on a string, going beyond the one-finger-per-fret span.

Example 2q is an eight-note diminished scale using four notes on one string. While it's technically possible to pivot your thumb or shift after the first two notes on each string, it's easier to play this using extended fingering. Start by placing your hand in 6th position, lining up your index finger with fret 6. Now, extend your index finger back to fret 5, then back up one fret to continue in position. Check the fingering in the notation if you're unsure.

Example 2q

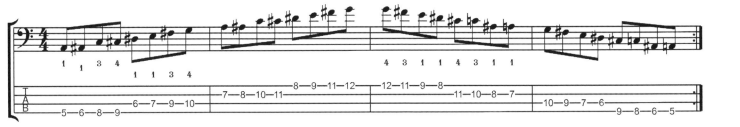

It's common for the index finger to stretch out, as in Example 2r. Look at this A Major scale in fourth position.

A Major in 4th Position

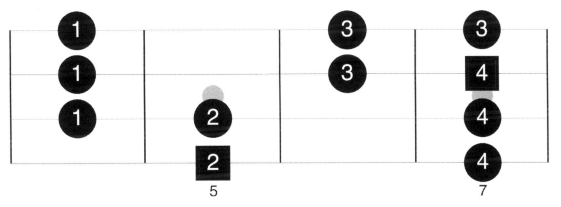

Now compare this pattern in sixth position. Notice that it's the index finger that stretches out of position. This is a good example of using extended fingering to increase the range. We'll revisit this technique later.

A Major in 6th Position – Three Notes Per String

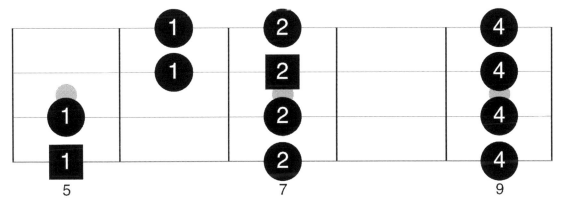

Example 2r ascends and descends this shape. When you play an extended fingering, you might need to shift your hand slightly to help you stretch out of the position.

Example 2r

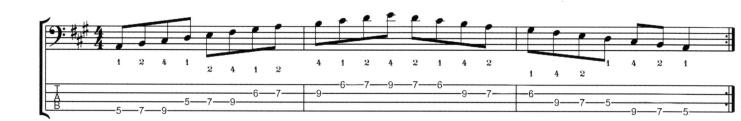

Here's an example bassline using the same pattern. There is a lot of scope for raking, rolling and fast alternate plucking in this pattern, so memorise it and use it to make your own lines and exercises.

Example 2s

Tone Is in The Hands

The sound you produce as a player depends on a lot of variables: the type of wood your bass is made from, the strings you use, your amp and how it's set up, effects pedals etc. However, you can alter your tone significantly just by using different hand placements and applying other fingerstyle techniques. We'll look at the most common methods in this section.

Plucking Hand Placement

Where you choose to pluck the strings will have a dramatic effect on the tone that is produced.

Plucking close to the bridge results in a tight, punchy sound. Jaco Pastorius' punchy, funky tone came from his plucking right over the bridge pickup.

Plucking over the end of the fretboard sounds brilliant for ballads, walking basslines and softer playing.

Playing halfway between the bridge and the neck gives a great lively rock sound.

In this section we'll look at each technique. All examples have a backing track, so you can experiment in context.

Example 3a is a funk line, so pluck this close to the bridge. Turn up the bridge pickup if you have one. If you only have one pickup, just listen to the tone difference that comes from plucking close to the bridge. You don't need to pluck as close as physically possible, just find the sweet spot for your bass, it may be an inch or two away.

Use your pinkie finger or ring finger to play the notes on fret 3 and keep the note lengths short.

Example 3a

Now pluck closer to the fretboard for this walking bassline over a 12-bar blues progression. You can even anchor your thumb on the top of the fretboard. Notice the huge difference in tone compared to plucking near the bridge.

Example 3b

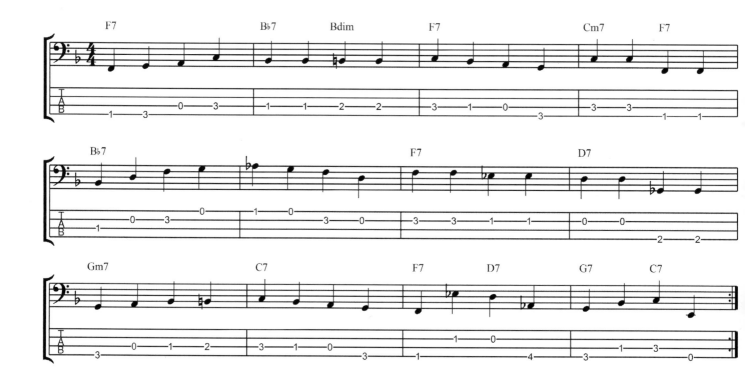

Example 3c is a rock line that requires some attitude and aggression. For this one, pluck in between the bridge and the neck. You can also experiment with really *digging in* and seeing how that affects the tone. Geddy Lee of Rush has a wonderful touch and his fingers strike the strings from a distance, producing a bright but meaty tone (working well with his overdrive). Still use rest strokes but strike the strings from a greater height. This attack will produce an authentic rock tone.

Example 3c

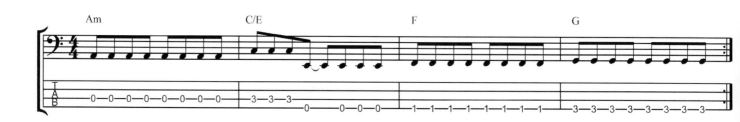

To recap, use whichever hand placement suits the style you're playing and the sound you want to make. You can also vary hand placement within a song. This is a great way of controlling dynamics, outlining sections and making your playing more interesting.

Dynamics

Dynamics refer to changes in playing volume or attack. They add interest, variety and musicality to your playing. Different sections of a song may change in intensity, or the singer may want to be more prominent in an especially tender moment – this is where dynamics come in. Learning how to control your volume with your touch is a crucial skill and it produces a different tone to just turning down the volume knob.

A great example of this is Jimmy Lee Moore's playing on *It's a Man's World* by James Brown. It's one of my favourite tunes and what strikes me more than anything is his masterful use of dynamics. I recommend you find it on YouTube and study his solo. Listen to how he makes full use of the bass' dynamic range.

In Example 3d the "*p*" stands for "piano" which means "quiet" or "softly". Typically, *piano* passages will be plucked nearer to the neck because of its naturally softer sound. The next three examples relate to each other and have backing tracks.

Example 3d

Pluck harder in the next example while keeping the 1/8th notes even with no change in tempo. There's a temptation to speed up when you dig in but listen to the drums and lock onto the high hat. The "*f*" means "forte" which means "loud" or "strong".

Example 3e

Now let's practice going from one section to the other and back again. Once you've practiced changing between *piano* and *forte* you can try using a *crescendo*. A crescendo is where you gradually get louder.

Example 3f

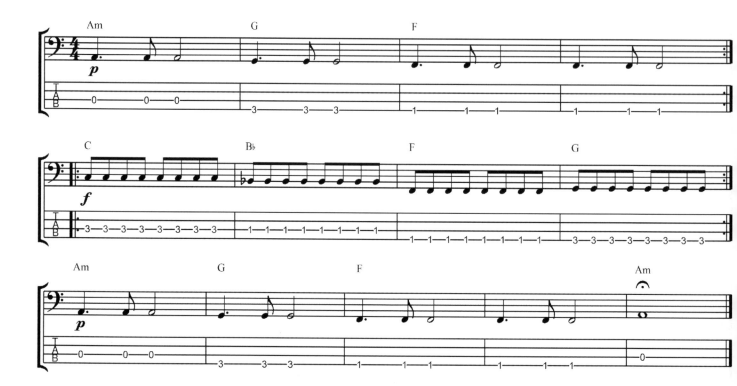

Earlier we used a middle hand placement to create a strong rock tone. We can get a more aggressive metal sound from this placement by attacking the strings from an even greater height. The angle and force you use to pluck can vastly change the dynamics and tone. Example 3g is a metal riff with the rhythms matched by the guitar and drums on the backing track. The rhythms are a little tricky so check the audio examples.

Since your plucking hand is a greater distance from the strings, use your fretting hand to mute and control note length. That hand has an important role to play in this line!

Example 3g

Palm Muting

Palm muting is a technique that uses the side of the plucking hand to imitate the sound of a mute. Old Fender basses used to have a foam mute attached to the underside of the bridge cover. This would gently touch the strings to create a mellow, thumping sound. The idea was to simulate the sound of an upright bass – it is not to be confused with the muting techniques we've already discussed which are designed to completely silence notes.

Most companies have now done away with the mute design, but we can still get the sound using our palms instead. First, make a karate chop shape with your hand. Place the fat side of your palm on the strings near the bridge then curl your fingers and bring your thumb down ready to pluck the strings, as illustrated below.

Any time you want to replicate that muffled, old school sound, you can use this technique. Here's a hip-hop line using palm muting (P.M.). Apply only a slight amount of pressure with the palm, too much will completely choke the note or push it out of tune.

Example 3h

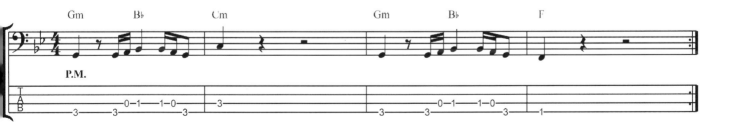

For this example, you'll need to move your palm mute depending on what strings you're plucking. Don't press down too hard on the D or G strings as you'll prevent them from vibrating. This one has a country style backing track.

Example 3i

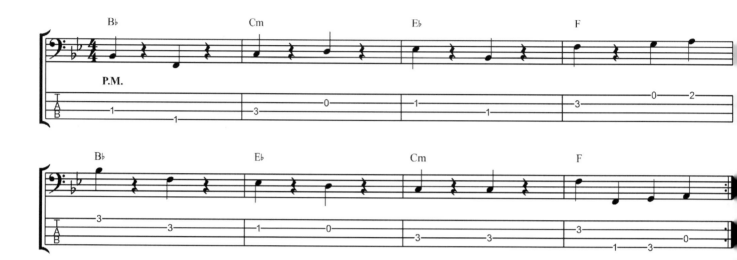

The fingers can also pluck in this position and will help with trickier passages like Example 3j. It's important to note that the fingers and thumb create different tones. The fingertips are smaller, and you might also catch the string with a nail, which makes a brighter sound. Also note that the lower your action (the height of your strings above the fretboard) the more difficult it is for the notes to ring out when palm muting. The "*p*" stands for "pulgar" (Latin for thumb) in the fingering guide.

Example 3j

The Fretting Hand Mute

This technique was pioneered by the late, great Francis Rocco Prestia. Listen to any Tower of Power record and you'll hear awesome 1/16th note basslines that sit perfectly in the mix. This is largely down to the incredible tone he gets from his left-hand muting.

The muting is done by the fingers not involved in fretting the note. Since the index and middle fingers are normally used to play the notes, the ring and pinkie fingers are free to mute. As with palm muting, you will gently touch the fingers on the string.

In Example 3k use the rolling technique to fret the 3rd fret with your index finger while flattening out your other fingers to mute.

Example 3k

Let's play the same thing with a different rhythm. Notice how the notes have a pleasing short length and a focused tone (one that cuts through nicely in a band or recording setting).

Example 3l

This technique requires you to shift your fretting hand rapidly as only the index and middle fingers are free to fret. This technique works extremely well with *ghost notes* (covered in the next section). Use the backing track for this 1/16th note line. Definitely check the audio example to hear the rhythms. Use your index finger to fret every note so you can mute with the remaining fingers.

Example 3m

Expressive Techniques

Expressive techniques or *articulations* bring life and flair to your playing. These expressive techniques will make your bass playing sound more sophisticated and will add colour to your playing. This section will teach you the main techniques and how to use them in your playing.

The Hammer-On

A *hammer-on* is when the fretting-hand produces a note without the plucking hand doing anything. The fretting hand finger hammers down onto a string with enough force to fret the note cause it to sound.

In Example 4a, use the index finger to fret the note on fret 5. Pluck the note, then hammer onto fret 6 with the middle finger.

Remember to keep your fretting hand fingers in their optimum position – playing on their tips with a slight curve. If you've not used this technique much in your playing thus far, it will also take some time to get a good hammer-on sound as you need to build up your fretting hand strength.

Once you have these elements in place, you'll realise that you don't need to hammer down from a great height and you can generate enough power hammering from a small distance. Think Bruce Lee's one inch punch!

Example 4a

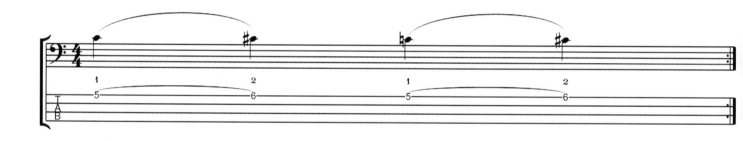

You can, and should be able to, hammer on using any finger. The next exercise incorporates hammer-ons with the middle, ring and pinkie fingers. A word of warning: the pinkie will feel the weakest by far but stick with it, the benefit to your all-round playing and fretting will be huge.

Example 4b

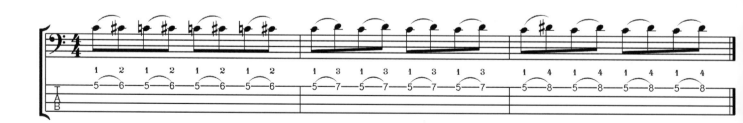

Due to the joints and tendons in the hand, hammer-ons between the index and ring, and middle and pinkie fingers will feel the most awkward. Many players avoid these altogether but let's take a look at an exercise to build it up instead of ignoring it!

Example 4c

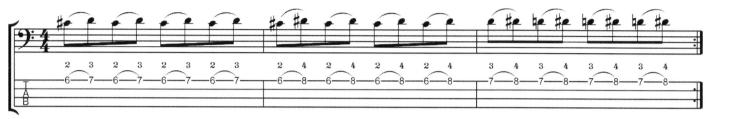

While the last three examples were great for introducing hammer-ons, they don't sound like real bass playing, so here's an A Minor Pentatonic scale using hammer-ons. Using pentatonic scales in particular is a good way to practice techniques while making music at the same time.

Example 4d

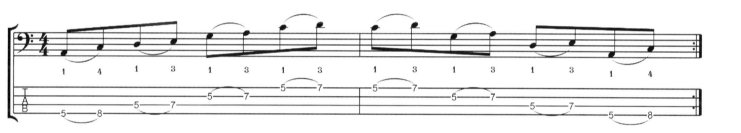

The next bassline uses the index finger to hammer-on. Developing your first-finger hammer-ons will free up the plucking hand. It also creates a different sound than plucking every single note (try it and compare).

Example 4e

The Pull-Off

A pull-off is essentially the opposite of a hammer-on and the two are often used in conjunction to create a *legato* (smooth) sound.

Look at the notation for Example 4f. Notice that pull-offs occur from a higher to a lower note, the opposite of a hammer-on. Have your index finger already fretting the 5th fret as you pluck the 7th. Then flick the ring finger down towards the floor. That flicking motion is the key to executing this technique perfectly. The flick acts like a pluck, but executed with a fretting hand finger.

Do not simply lift up your finger. This is a common mistake. It just doesn't generate any force on the string and results in a limp, sad note! Return your ring finger to position as soon as it has flicked the string.

Focus on getting the timing as close to perfect as possible. This might mean starting at a much lower metronome setting than you think.

Example 4f

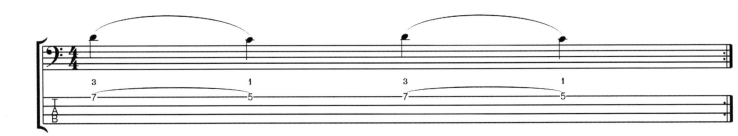

Keep your index finger on the 5th fret throughout the next example. This one shows how useful the one-finger-per-fret technique can be.

Example 4g

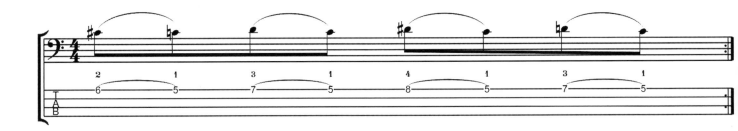

Let's now test those awkward tendons in the middle, ring and pinkie fingers. This time you'll keep your middle finger down on fret 6. Be sure not to drag that finger down so it slips off the string. You can twist the wrist a little, keeping the thumb at the back of the neck, when pulling off with the pinkie finger.

Example 4h

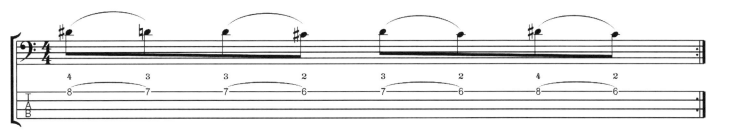

Most bassists, including myself, find pull-offs harder than hammer-ons when crossing strings. This next exercise will help you to master this situation. Take it slowly and pay very close attention to your index finger. While you fret the higher note, you actually have slightly more time than you think to get the index finger into position for the pull-off.

Once you get used to this example, randomly change the order to create different patterns.

This example uses hammer-ons and pull-offs in a bassline. Unlike the exercises in previous chapters, here the fretting hand is responsible for much of the rhythmic interest. Watch out for the shift in bar four and use the backing drum beat to keep you accountable with the rhythm.

Example 4i

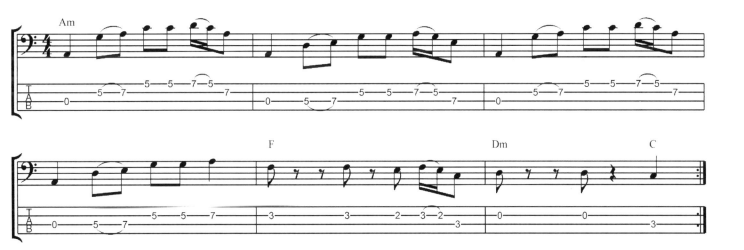

Bends

String bending is a technique where you use more than one finger to deliberately stretch the string to a higher pitch. Usually, it's a half or whole step but it's possible to bend higher than that.

The technique requires a little more strength in the fretting hand than you usually need. It also requires more coordination. Normally, we are just working to push the string in towards the fretboard. When bending, we have to apply downward pressure and push into the direction of the bend (see picture below). This extra coordination takes time to get consistent, so be patient and don't overwork yourself.

Example 4j is a half-step bend at the 14th fret. Bending near the midpoint of the string is much easier than near the nut, so this is a great place to start.

First, fret the note on the 15th fret, just to get used to the sound of the note you're aiming for when you bend. Then place your middle and ring fingers side by side on the fret below. You can put your thumb over the top of the neck then squeeze, pushing the string into the fretboard and upwards.

Example 4j

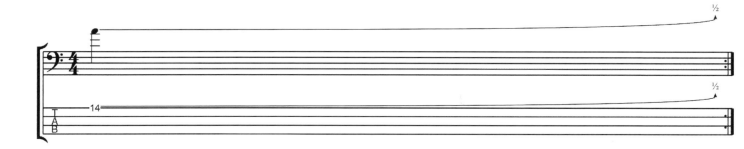

There are lots of different types of bend. One is called a *bend and release*. It's the same as the previous example, except that after completing the bend, you release the bend and return to the original pitch. Listen to the audio example to catch the difference.

Example 4k

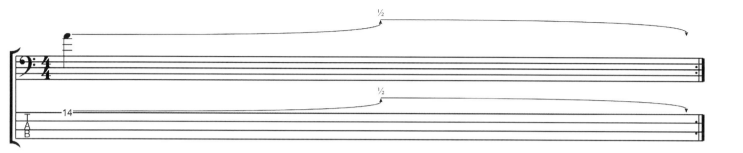

Another cool bending technique is the *pre-bend and release*. This time, bend the note a half step before plucking. Once you are roughly in position, pluck then release the bend. Don't worry if you're not bang on pitch, after a while you'll develop the muscle memory to be able to do this accurately.

Example 4l

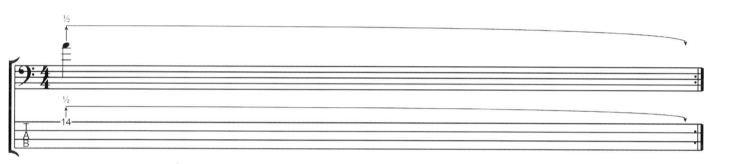

As you might have realised, whole-step bends are harder to play than half-step bends. You may not quite have enough strength to execute this properly, or your bass may be set up in such a way as to make it virtually impossible. Lighter gauge strings and a lower action definitely help.

You'll need to apply a lot more pressure here, so hook that thumb over the top of the neck to help. Example 4m uses some full bends (as they're sometimes called) with the E Minor Pentatonic scale for some bluesy lines.

Example 4m

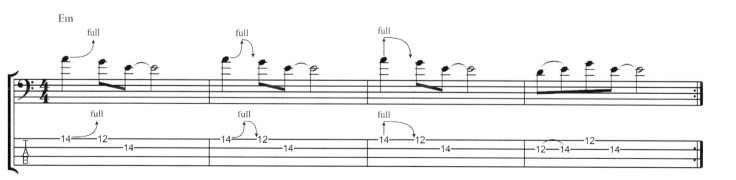

So far, we've looked at bends where the string is pushed upwards. If you're bending the E string, you can't push it up, so you will need to do the opposite movement. Bring your middle and ring fingers together and pull downwards. It's a little easier as the E string is under less tension.

In the next example, pay attention to the amount of pressure you need to exert for the different bends. Listen to the audio example to hear the correct pitches.

Example 4n

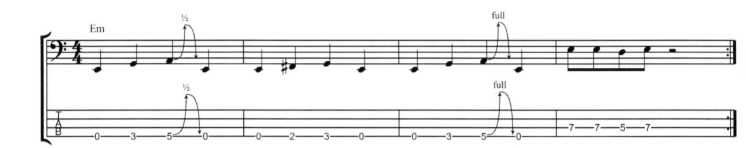

Slides

There are two main ways in which slides are commonly used in bass playing. The first is where a slide is used as a percussive/sonic effect, for instance to slide into a section of a song. One example of this is when the bass comes in during the intro to *Smells Like Teen Spirit* by Nirvana. The other type of slide is used as a fill, in a solo to connect notes, or as part of the bassline itself. Paul McCartney's genius bassline in *Come Together* springs to mind.

Regardless of the context, the same technique is used. Fret the string and shift your hand higher or lower on the neck *without* releasing too much pressure. A common mistake I see students make is to immediately release all pressure with the fretting hand fingers and stop the note.

Remember that good technique is about control of the instrument and sliding requires complete control.

There are two types of slide: a *legato slide* and *shift slide*. With a legato slide, a note is plucked once and then you slide to another note. A shift slide is the same except you re-pluck when you get to the destination note. Example 4o shows the different notation for the slides.

Use your index or middle finger to fret the 3rd fret note, then slide up one octave to the 15th. Don't pluck the high G in the first bar, but do in the second.

Don't pay much attention to the speed at the moment, just make sure the fretting hand pressure is correct so that the note doesn't die out. Release enough pressure so that your thumb isn't getting stuck and you can glide up the neck.

Example 4o

You can also *slide-in* to a note from below or above. This is one of my favourite techniques on bass and it adds real panache to blues, funk, pop and rock playing. The thumb pivot is often the key to making this technique sound smooth.

Notice in Example 4p that there's no starting note written for the slide. This is because the initial note doesn't have any duration, you are simply sliding in from below. Where you chose to start that slide depends on what texture you want to create.

Use your ring finger for both slides in the next example and pivot your thumb when you slide up. You can then return to the thumb's normal position or even shift a little if you need to. Use the rolling technique with the index finger for the notes on the 5th fret.

Example 4p

Legato slides are probably the most common and are especially useful when playing up and down one string. Marcus Miller uses this technique a lot. Work through Example 4q following the notation exactly, then come up with your own lines using the following ideas:

- Create patterns and move through them sequentially (e.g. up two notes, down one)

- Vary the rhythms

- Play your A string as a continuous drone while improvising with the scale on the G string. This will get your ear used to the sound of the scale

- Do the same with different scales and even on different strings

Example 4q

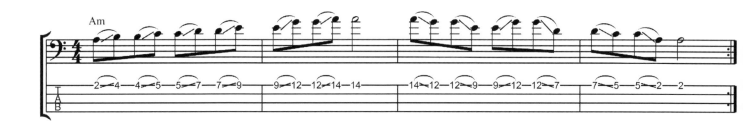

The next example is a melodic pop line where the slides add a soulful, vocal quality to the bassline. Pivot your thumb for the fill in bar two and use your ring finger to slide up and back again. Listen to the audio example for the rhythm and check out the backing track.

Example 4r

Ghost Notes

Ghost notes create percussive, funky, rhythmic sounds. Indeed, they are found more in funk music than any other style but, applied subtly, can be used in most styles.

Fret any note then release pressure while still touching the string. Now pluck and you will hear a dead, drum-like tone. If you are hearing a slight harmonic, it's because one finger is a bit close to a *node* (the point on a string where harmonics can be produced). You can solve this problem by using more than one finger to dampen the string. You can even use all four fingers straightened out.

Example 4s uses ghost notes (notated with an x). Listen to the audio and you'll hear that the ghost notes create a rhythm within the bassline.

When playing this line, watch out for the F octaves in bar four. Have your pinkie (or ring) finger ready to fret the octave while your middle finger plucks the first F in bar four.

Example 4s

Here's a soul bassline that uses ghost notes. Use the rolling technique for the notes on the same fret and the remaining fingers to mute the strings for the ghost notes. Then concentrate on lifting those fingers off so the fretted notes can sound.

Example 4t

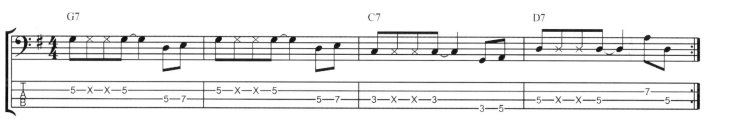

Ghost notes work especially well in 1/16th note lines. It takes a bit of focus to coordinate both hands, so slow right down to work on this. The audio example is slowed right down so you can hear where the ghost notes lie.

Example 4u

Vibrato

On stringed instruments, *vibrato* is used to emulate the soul and emotion of the human voice. There are two main ways to perform vibrato. The first and most subtle is to move the string parallel to its axis by gently wiggling your finger from side to side. The other is to bend the string slightly and bring it back to pitch repeatedly.

The first type is called *axial* vibrato and the second *radial*. Both methods bring the note in and out of pitch, simulating the musical sound vocalists often use on longer notes. It is a beautiful sound in the correct context.

Bending the string up and down is the easiest one to do on bass. How much you move up and down (depth) and how fast (rate) is down to personal preference and the musical situation, but as a general rule, a subtle vibrato tends to suit most situations. Rock and metal bass playing often uses fast, wide vibrato. There's a good example of this in the intro of *King for a Day* by Faith No More.

Experiment with radial and axial vibrato, adjusting the depth and rate throughout the next few examples. You may want to use the middle and ring fingers together to assist with the bending element.

The next example has a slow, chilled backing track. Repeat the example, altering the vibrato until you find the method that suits your style. It's a really personal thing, so go with what sounds right to you. It's one of those situations where there's a lot of room for interpretation, so spend some time on this.

Example 4v

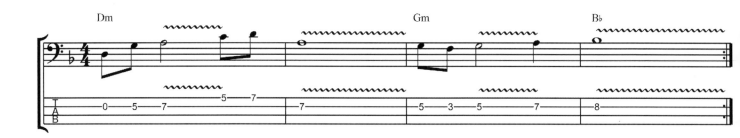

There are times when you can be more aggressive with your vibrato, as in the next example. Use your ring and pinkie fingers to bend the string up and down. Go for it with this one – you really can't overdo it! Play along with the backing track.

Example 4w

Combining Elements

To conclude this section on expressive techniques, here are three exercises that combine traditional legato techniques. Remember that *legato* means "smooth" in Italian and we want to achieve an even flow of notes when we play. This short section concentrates on combining hammer-ons, pull-offs and slides to achieve a great legato feel.

Use this first exercise to get used to the added fretting hand workload. It's a little harder on the way down with pull-offs so focus on that section. Feel free to use your index finger to rake while descending but use alternate plucking on the way up.

Example 4x

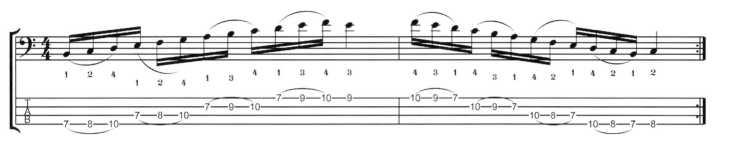

Although extremely fast, fluid lines can be created using legato technique, legato doesn't have to equal speed. You can create wonderfully fluid lines with it and the next example adds some slides into the mix. Build this line up piece by piece and follow the fingerings and notation/TAB exactly. The slide is carried out by the index finger.

This kind of line tests your coordination like no other, so play through it very slowly taking care that the plucking pattern you use complements the legato.

Example 4y

Here's one more bassline that uses slides, hammer-ons and pull-offs. Notice how different the feel is when you use these techniques to create a legato sound, rather than a fully plucked tone. Slide into the 7th fret from two frets below and shift your hand quickly as you do so.

Example 4z

Building Speed

Playing fast is a central goal for many bass players. After all, who isn't impressed by someone burning up and down the neck at ferocious speeds? This chapter will cover the basics of how to build speed, as well as some useful techniques that will make playing at high speeds much easier.

How to Develop Speed

The key to playing fast is simple yet extremely unintuitive:

To play fast you must first play slow

Memorise that and never forget it.

To build up the neural connections and form the myelin in the brain that binds a good habit, you need to play at slow tempos and gradually build up to playing fast. If you do this, what can be achieved is nothing short of remarkable.

A big mistake is to run before you can walk, to try and play up to speed when you're not ready. This could be linked to a lack of patience or simply not knowing how speed is built.

Any exercise can be used to develop speed but here are the ones that I have found to be the most effective.

Example 5a is a cyclical pattern of 1/16th notes. This will build your plucking speed as well as your ability to quickly cross strings. Remember our new mantra and start it at a slow, easily manageable pace. Use one finger per fret and alternate plucking for this example.

Example 5a

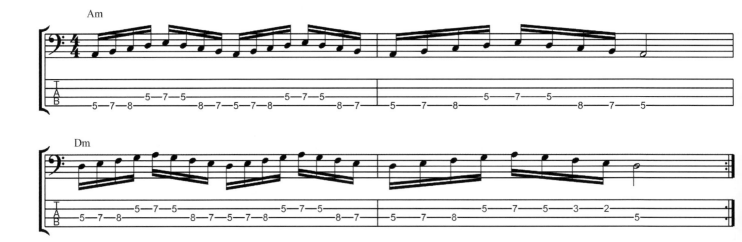

Now let's use an A Major scale applying the same idea of starting slow and gradually building up. At 60BPM the 1/16th notes are more than manageable. Concentrate on the notes flowing smoothly and seamlessly into each other. Once you are comfortable, build up the tempo in increments of no more than 5BPM. At the point where the tempo becomes too fast to play the exercise cleanly, stop and make a note of the BPM. This is your new benchmark to work on for tomorrow.

As much as anything, you are training yourself to be patient. You want to play fast as soon as possible, but be disciplined and trust the process!

Example 5b

Here's the same exercise, this time ascending through the modes of C Major. Concentrate on making quick position shifts during the rests. For a little variety, try altering the rhythm and even the order of the notes.

Example 5c

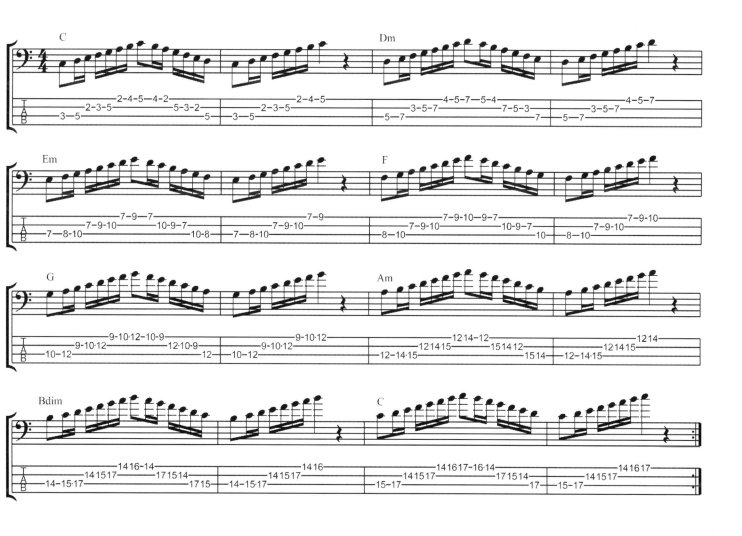

Now let's play a few basslines that call for some fast fingers. Example 5d is a 160BPM rock line. Remember that down in first position, you can use your pinkie finger on the 3rd fret if it's more comfortable. Or you can start in second position, then shift to the 1st fret with your first finger. Remember our mantra for building speed and aim to play this perfectly over the backing track in due course.

Example 5d

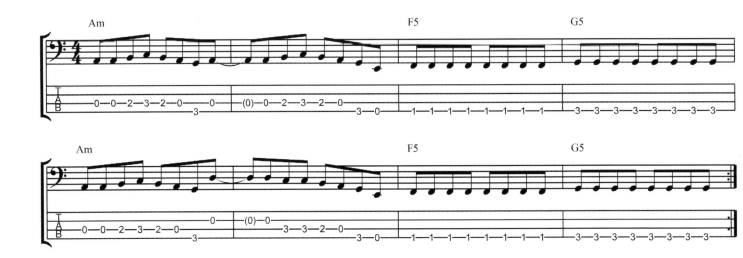

Funk bass playing often features precisely plucked, syncopated lines. In the next example, focus on the hand shift between bars one and two. Play along to the backing track. Be sure to keep the 1/8th notes short using muting. (For more funk basslines take a look at my book *100 Funk Bass Grooves for Electric Bass*).

Example 5e

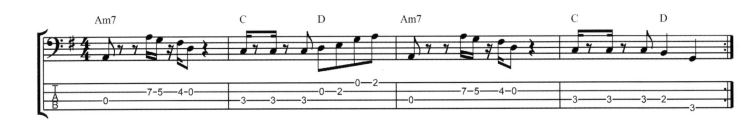

Here's a line with an octave jump followed by some 1/16th notes. This exercise presents you with some challenging string skipping. The pattern is the same throughout, so figure it out slowly then play to the backing track when you have it up to speed. Use the suggested plucking directions in bar one throughout.

Example 5f

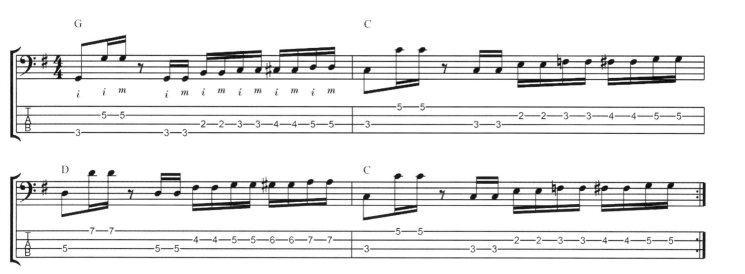

Three Finger Plucking

One way to increase your potential plucking speed is to introduce an extra finger and use the ring finger as well as the index and middle. To introduce you to this technique we are going to use a *gallop*. This is a rhythm made famous by Steve Harris of Iron Maiden and sounds like a galloping horse.

The rhythm is an 1/8th note followed by two 1/16th notes. First, let's use the traditional alternate plucking approach. Notice how you start on a different finger each time.

Example 5g

Example 5h has a slightly different plucking pattern. Notice how the index finger lands on all the 1/8th note beats. This makes the whole line sound much smoother and has more consistent dynamics.

Example 5h

The last way to play this figure is to use three fingers on the plucking hand. Using the ring finger (notated with an "*a*" for "annular" – Latin for "ring") can make playing this line much easier, but it will take some time to get comfortable. It can feel weird at first and you may also need to alter your hand position slightly.

Example 5i

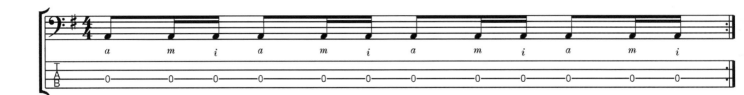

Use the next example and backing track to practice the three plucking patterns above. Pay attention to the different feel each plucking pattern produces. You can choose how to incorporate each one into your style of playing. This line will build up your plucking stamina, but remember to take a break if you experience any pain.

Example 5j

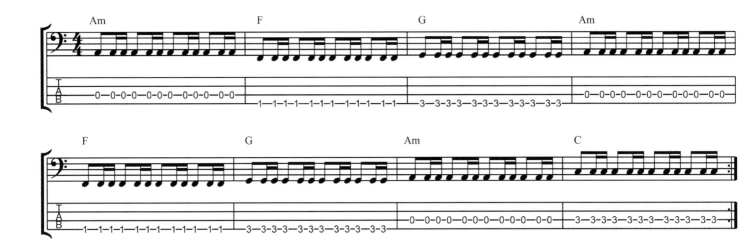

Three Notes Per String

In order to play fast passages on bass, it's important to construct basslines in the most efficient way possible. You can master the art of rapid plucking with the plucking hand, but if you are fingering phrases awkwardly with the fretting hand, this will be a limiting factor.

When it comes to playing scales on bass, the three-note-per-string system is by far the most efficient way. The patterns fall under the fingers naturally and can therefore be played quickly. It's the scale system of choice for players who want to play at high speeds, but it's also a very simple way to learn the fretboard and makes things at slower speeds seem even easier.

Space won't allow an in-depth look at every type of scale/pattern, but I'll demonstrate the three-note-per-string shapes for the major scale here and show you how they can be used in musical situations.

There are seven different positions for the major scale, one starting on each scale degree. Here are all the three-note-per-string patterns for the A Major scale. The square notes represent the root of the scale. Memorising the position of the root notes will allow you to move these shapes to other keys.

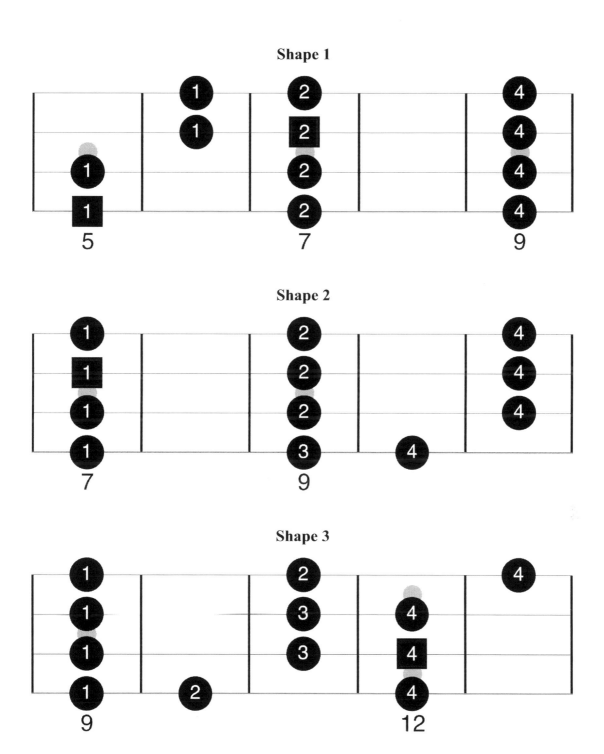

Shape 1

Shape 2

Shape 3

Shape 4

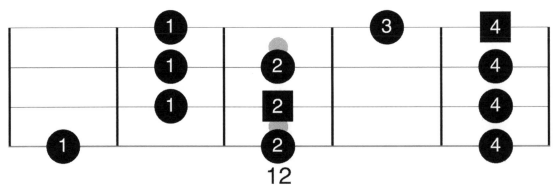

12

Shape 5

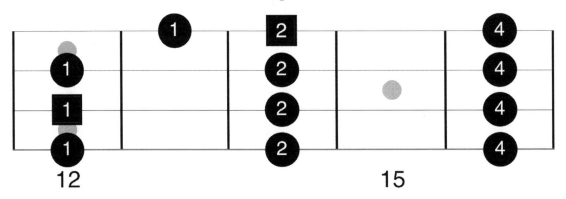

12   15

Shape 6

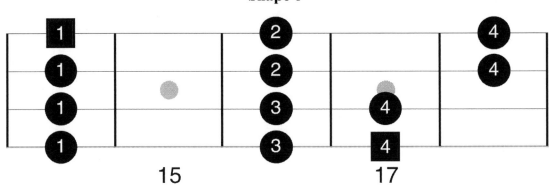

15   17

Shape 7

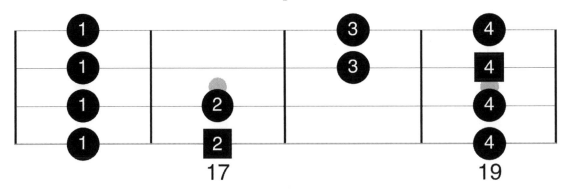

17   19

Committing these shapes to memory will help you to learn the fretboard, improvise, and write great basslines.

Example 5k uses the third shape which sits under the fingers easily. You'll notice the gallop again here. Make sure to prepare your plucking finger for the string jump in the second bar (remember the *one finger in the future* technique). Get the right rocky tone by plucking in the middle position and attacking the strings from higher than normal.

Example 5k

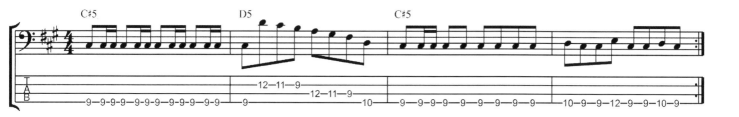

The next example uses the first shape and requires some extended fingering. This shape opens up the fretboard allowing for a creative fill at the end with no shifting. As soon as you've finished playing the A note on fret 5, relax your hand back into sixth position (first finger lining up with fret 6) before stretching out again on the repeat.

Example 5l

The following Rush-inspired example shifts between two shapes, so get your fretting hand ready for the move. Listen to the audio example for the rhythms as there are a couple of ties which may catch you out. Try tapping your foot on the beat if you need help accurately hitting the notes on the up beat.

Example 5m

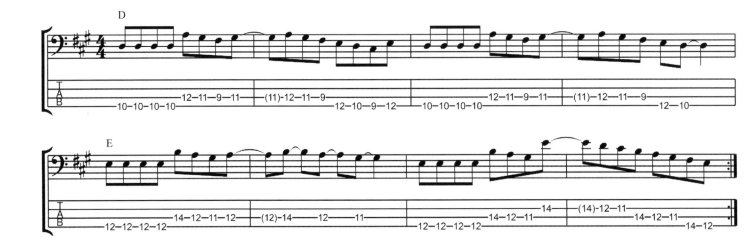

1/16th Note Triplets

If ever you've heard a piece of seriously fast playing, this is often achieved with 1/16th note triplets. These are the rhythmic big guns. Most pieces of music won't have rhythmic subdivisions smaller than 1/16th note triplets – in fact, most songs don't go past regular 1/16th notes.

If 1/16th notes looked a little scary on paper, these will look positively terrifying. But don't worry, because as ever, slowing things down reveals the truth that it's not as bad as you thought.

I recommend setting your metronome to 60BPM or lower while you work to bring these up to speed. Listen closely to the audio examples and notice how naturally six notes per beat works with the three-notes-per-string system.

Example 5n plays through different rhythms at slow tempos. You need to *internalise* the feeling of 1/16th note triplets, as you would any other rhythm. Aim to feel two groups of three notes per beat. Only when you are comfortable should you work these up to speed. There's zero benefit in speeding up if it doesn't sound tight at a much slower tempo. Be patient.

Take this same exercise and work it through the other three-note-per-string patterns. This exercise might look quite challenging but trust me, if you slow it down and practice diligently, you'll nail it. To help you, I've created a video demonstration which you can see here: **https://www.fundamental-changes.com/bass-videos**

Example 5n

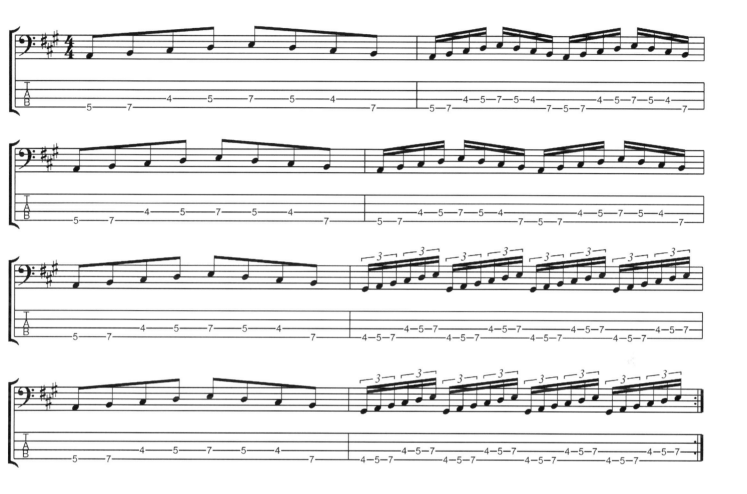

Here's the rhythm in a musical context. Example 5o uses the F# Natural Minor scale in a rock style. You will need to keep the index and middle fingers alternating to make it work. Notice how it's actually more beneficial *not* to use an open string in this example.

Example 5o

Jazz often uses fast triplet rhythms. Listen to Jaco Pastorius playing *Donna Lee* for a great example. In a jazz swing setting, they are notated as in the following example and are similar to 1/16th note triplets. There are three in every beat. Listen to the audio example to catch the swing rhythm. This one's a good workout for the ring and pinkie fingers.

Example 5p

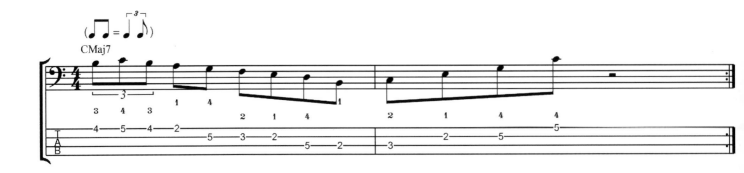

Chordal Playing

A chord is simply multiple notes played simultaneously and on bass is quite a specialised technique. Although you probably won't play chords often (unless you play progressive music or solo bass), there's still a lot of benefit to practicing them. Understanding chords can help your composition, improvisation, fretboard knowledge and aural skills. It can also expand your creativity.

This section will teach you the techniques required to play chords, as well as a few of the most common shapes you can improvise and compose with. They're fun to practice and a good way to increase your musicality and theory knowledge.

Free Strokes

The technique required to play chords uses a different type of stroke to the rest stroke. A *free stroke* involves plucking the string slightly away from the body of the bass. This means you're not resting a finger on the string below after plucking, allowing the chord to ring out.

When plucking chords, we add the thumb (*p* for "pulgar" – Latin for "thumb") to the index and middle fingers. In general, each digit is allocated its own string.

Let's get used to this new technique with Example 6a. As with rest strokes, this type of fingerstyle benefits from anchoring. You can gently rest your pinkie against the body of the bass and/or your wrist on the upper body as in the image below.

When playing free strokes, don't let your finger and thumb tips travel too far after you pluck. You want them to be able to reset quickly, ready for the next stroke. Allow the notes to ring out but make sure to mute the A and E to stop the note after four beats.

When you pluck the notes of a chord separately like this it's called *arpeggiating*.

Example 6a

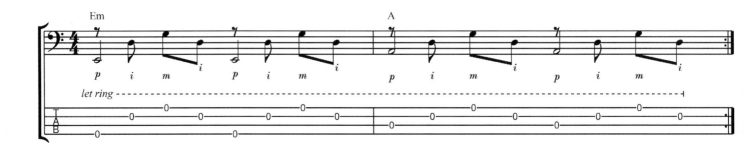

You can also pluck notes together at the same time as in the next example.

Example 6b

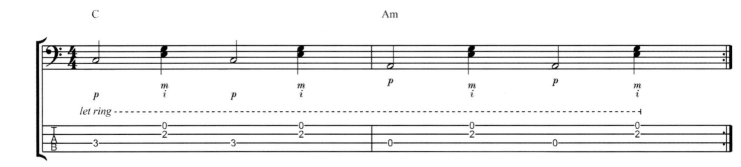

Now that we have the necessary technique, we can learn some chord *voicings*. Chord voicings or "shapes" are similar to scales in that you can move them to different frets and suddenly know twelve chords for the price of one. Here are the shapes for the seventh chords of the C Major scale on the A string.

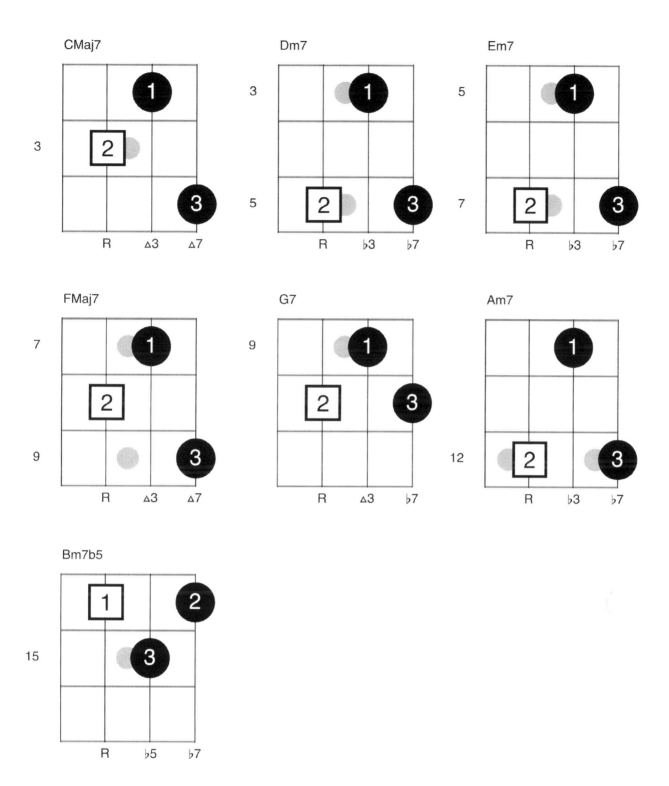

You can make so much music just from these shapes! Example 6c uses the first, third and second chord. Musicians label them with Roman numerals using upper case for major chords and lower case for minor, like this:

C	Dm	Em	F	G	Am	Bdim
I	ii	iii	IV	V	vi	vii

So, Example 6c can be described as a I iii ii progression in the key of C Major. It's a way of quickly describing the chord changes in any key. I recommend you get this lingo down as musicians use it all the time.

Use the backing track to make up your own rhythms, changing the order in which you pluck the notes and pluck with thumb, index and middle fingers respectively.

Example 6c

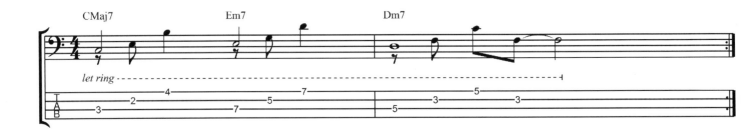

Example 6d uses a pretty sounding progression using major sevenths.

Example 6d

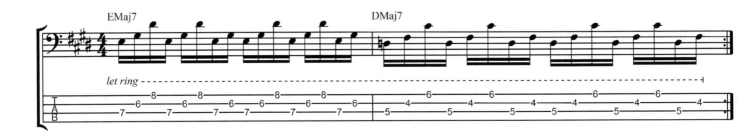

The next example uses seventh chords to create a bossa nova style bassline. You might need to piece this one together bit by bit. The thumb outlines a simple root-fifth bassline while the fingers pluck a cool rhythm. Go through the first bar slowly, the rhythms and plucking patterns are then the same throughout.

Example 6e

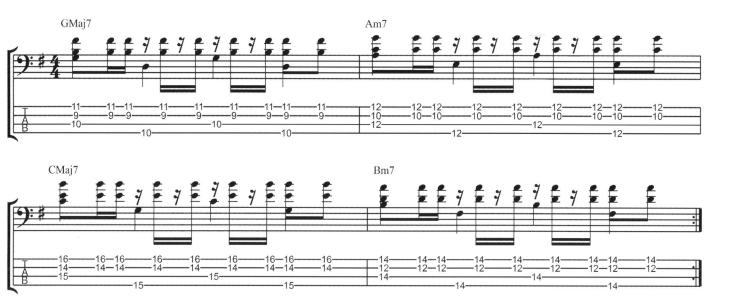

The sus2 chord shape below works over both major and minor chords, since there's no third to define the quality. You can move this shape around on the E and A strings and it's fantastic for pop and rock (remember that you can also play the notes separately and use them in basslines and fills).

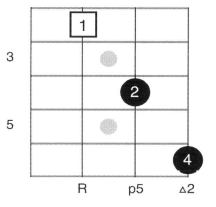

Where the root note is on the E string, the gap between the fingers is a little wider, so take care with those ones. Keep the hand shifts smooth and swift and use the fingering pattern in bar one. You can use your ring instead of middle finger if it's more comfortable, but notice how the suggested way uses extended fingering. It's good to get used to this stretch, it will definitely help you in the long run.

Example 6f

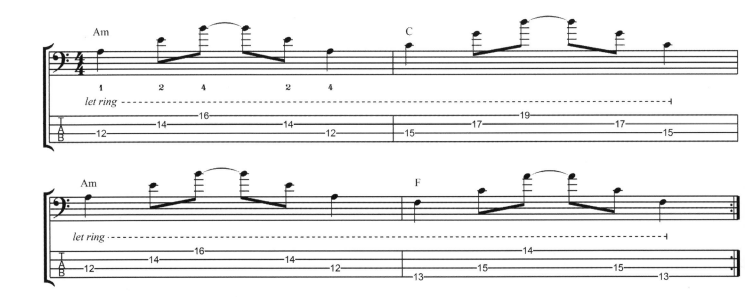

Barring

A barre makes it easier to hold chords that have notes on the same fret, just like the rolling technique. To play a barre you straighten your first finger across the neck, causing it to act like a new nut.

Example 6g uses major and minor chords with roots on the E string. The minor chord is the one that needs to be barred. Fret the E note on the 12th fret with your first fingertip then flatten out your finger so that the knuckle pushes down on the G string, 12th fret.

This would be a great chord progression to lay down on a loop pedal, then try soloing over it with the E Natural Minor scale. Use the same plucking pattern throughout and listen to the audio example for the tempo.

Example 6g

Double-Stops

A double-stop is where you play just two notes at the same time. They are used a lot in conventional bass playing. Excellent examples include Tony Levin's bassline on *Don't Give Up* by Peter Gabriel and countless basslines by Chuck Rainey. My favourite is *Peg* by Steely Dan which has a lovely double-stop in the intro, and Bobby Watson sneaks one in the middle eight of *Rock With You* by Michael Jackson. That one gets me every time!

There are a few ways to play them. One is to pluck a bass note using a rest stroke, then play the double-stop using free strokes. In the next example, make sure you curl the fingers as you pluck the double-stops, so you don't accidentally hit (and stop) the open string ringing out. Use your index and middle fingers to fret the notes.

Example 6h

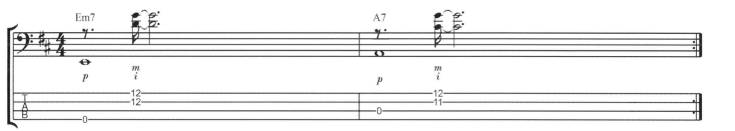

The next example is a bass groove ending with a double-stop. Fret the notes of the double-stop with your first finger. Use the backing track to work this up to speed.

Example 6i

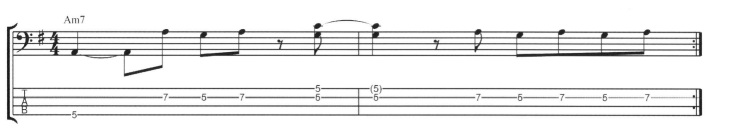

Make sure you follow the recommended fingering for the next example. That way you will always have fretting hand fingers ready for the next notes. Make sure those fingers are hovering over the double-stops *before* you pluck them. Use rest strokes for the single notes and free strokes for the double-stops. You'll notice a quick hand shift when you jump to pluck the double-stops, so look out for that.

Example 6j

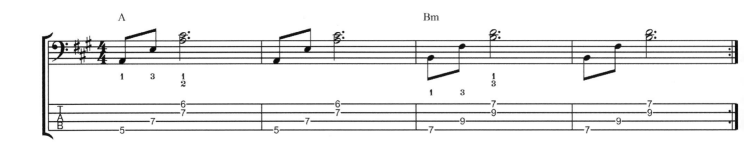

Putting It All Together

Everything you've learnt up to this point will set you up perfectly for a whole range of musical and playing styles. Should you want to move on to more advanced styles, play with a plectrum, or develop your slap playing, you now have a rock-solid foundation from which to do so.

This final section brings together all the techniques you have learnt and puts them to work in real world musical situations and has three longer pieces for you to play, each with a backing track. Each piece is first broken down into individual sections, each with its own audio example. The aim is for you to master the component parts, then play each whole piece flawlessly from beginning to end using the backing track.

The intro section of the first piece is all about the note lengths and how you control them with your fretting hand. The 1/16th notes use hammer-ons so your fingers will need to be quick there. Use your ring or pinkie finger for fret 4, whichever you feel most comfortable with.

Example 7a

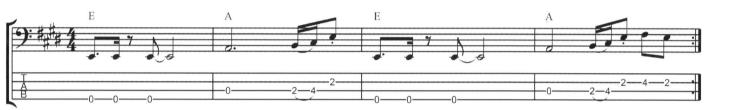

The next example features syncopated rhythms so listen to the audio example if you're unsure. Everything is played in one position apart from the fill in bar four. For that, you need to shift your hand quickly up two frets.

Example 7b

Example 7c looks easy but don't be fooled; playing 1/8th notes perfectly in time without rushing is anything but. I've indicated the fingers I use for the run in the last bar. Since I often use my pinkie finger in place of my ring finger to minimise the stretch in that area of the neck, I then shift briefly to use my index and middle fingers before returning to the 4th fret with my pinkie.

If you want, you can use the one-finger-per-fret technique instead, keeping your index finger hovering over the 1st fret.

Example 7c

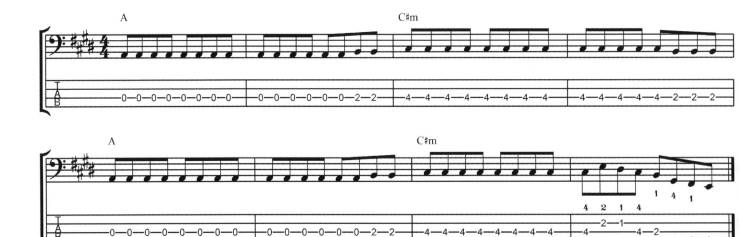

Things get more interesting in this section. The slide to the 9th fret requires a quick hand shift. Give the note a little vibrato when you get there before returning down the neck for the pull-off. Use two fingers for the bend in bar four and concentrate on the large shift back down to the 2nd fret.

Example 7d

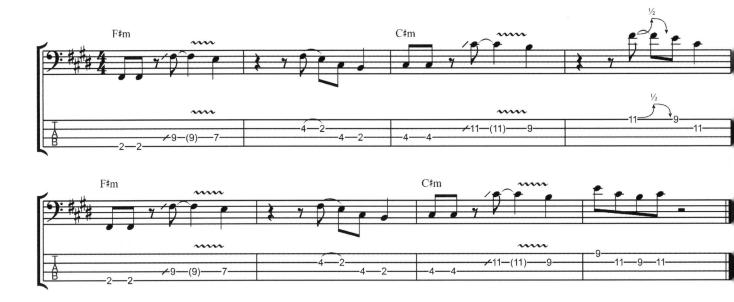

You can practice your rolling and raking in the next example. Make sure the notes don't bleed into each other and be aware of the rhythms by counting in 1/16ths as you go. This is a really common root, fifth, octave pattern. It's used in a lot of basslines so it's worth getting it under your fingers.

Example 7e

The outro features more hammer-ons and pull-offs using 1/16th notes and a sliding line before the last bar. When you get to the open strings in bar three, shift your hand up ready to play the 9th fret. You can use your first or second finger to play all the notes in that bar. These are legato slides so remember to pluck then slide and repeat that motion.

Example 7f

Work on each section until you're comfortable and then play the whole thing with the backing track.

The second piece contains four sections, one of which is repeated.

Example 7g uses octaves which require constant and steady hand shifts. Again, use your pinkie finger to fret the octave to lessen the stretch. Aim to maintain that hand shape as you move, only adjusting slightly as the fret spacings change. That way, your hand is already in position to play the next octave pattern. Use index then middle fingers to pluck the octaves. The tricky bit is in the last bar, so isolate the fill and follow the notation/ TAB exactly.

Example 7g

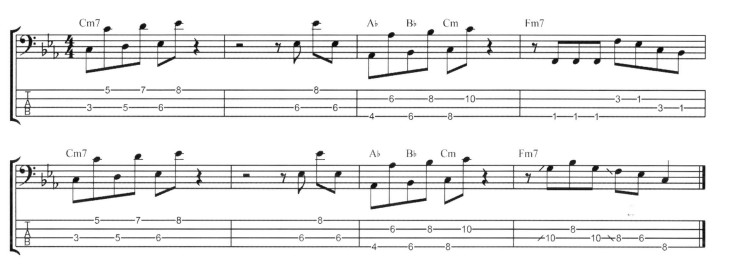

You might need to listen to the audio to get the syncopated rhythms in the next example. It's the same rhythm in each bar though, so once you crack it, you'll be fine. The challenging part here is controlling the note lengths with the left hand and keeping the plucking strictly alternate.

Example 7h

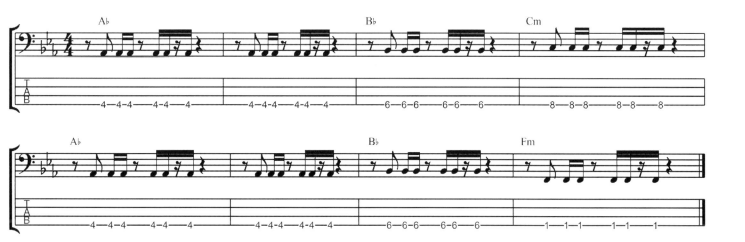

The next section of the piece is a repeat of Example 7g. Then the same chord progression as Example 7h comes in with a different rhythm and a fill, shown in Example 7i. The overall key of the piece is C minor, so you can use the C Natural Minor scale for fills and embellishments. Use the following scale pattern and try making up your own fills. They tend to sound best at the end of a phrase (bar four in this case). Make sure that on the repeat, you land on the Ab note on beat one.

C Natural Minor

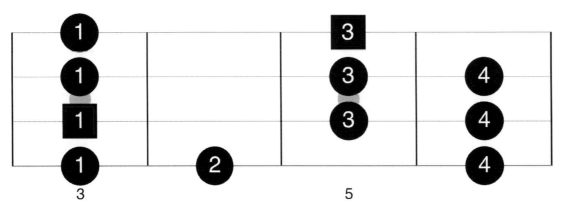

Example 7i

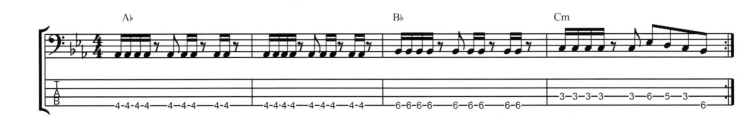

The only thing to watch for in the outro section is the lead up to the slide in the last bar. A good place to slide down, away from a note, is on the end note of a song. Used occasionally it sounds really cool. To get a proper slide in, the C note needs to be played on fret 8 rather than fret 3 of the A string. Where you choose to play a note can help or hinder your technical and expressive options. The suggested fingering requires a quick shift between frets 4 and 6. You're then in position for the slide.

Example 7j

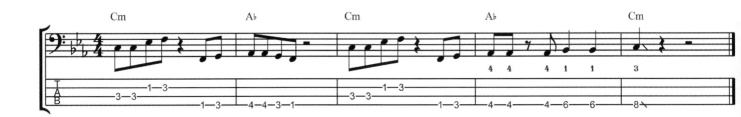

When you're ready, try the full piece.

The final piece is a minor 12-bar blues in 12/8 time. For this time signature, you still feel four beats in a bar but each beat is split into three 1/8th notes. This creates a shuffle feel that you'll quickly pick up when you hear the audio example.

The bassline itself is fairly straightforward. Follow the notation/TAB and the audio example and you'll have it in no time. This piece is all about you putting the techniques from this book into practice then using them to make up your own music.

Memorise the chord progression and then use the notes of the G Minor Blues scale (shown below) to improvise your own lines and fills. Stick to simple rhythms and short runs. You can start by replacing some of the existing notes with different ones from the diagram below. You'll soon be using your ear to find what works. You can even take a solo just by using the notes of the scale.

A helpful tip is to start paying attention to what interval of a scale you're playing at any given time (intervals are indicated on the diagram). As you practice, train your ears to hear the sounds and qualities these intervals contain.

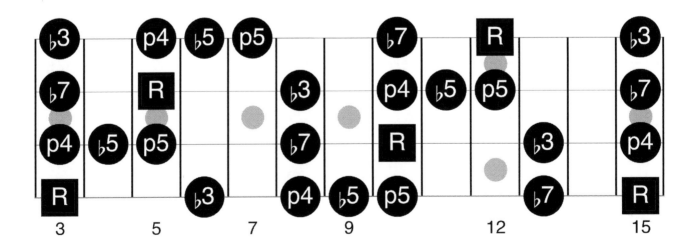

As every chord is a minor chord, you can move this scale shape onto each root and use it to further develop your lines. The roots are found as follows:

- Gm – 3rd fret E string

- Cm - 3rd fret A string

- Dm – 5th fret A string

Another melodic option is the minor pentatonic scale shown below. Notice that all the notes of the minor seventh arpeggio are right there within it. This makes it a very strong option to use in your lines. You can really go for it with these shapes and use all kinds of articulations and rhythms to inspire you.

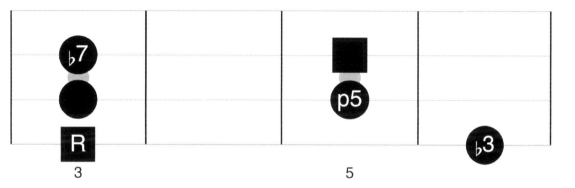

I've created a video lesson to give you plenty of ideas and to explain this idea more fully. Check it out here: **https://www.fundamental-changes.com/bass-videos**

Immerse yourself in this blues progression until you've memorised it. Then play along to the backing track and improvise using the patterns above. Work on incorporating new techniques, rhythms and scales into your playing.

Example 7k

Gear Tips

Hopefully this book has helped you gain an excellent foundation for bass technique which will give you the ability to play any musical genre you want with ease. However, there's nothing worse than struggling along with an instrument that is difficult to play. I've seen people give up far too early simply because they were fighting a bass that was practically unplayable. It's worth stacking the odds in your favour by choosing the right instrument for you and getting it set up to your exact preference.

What bass?

Everyone has different sized hands and if you find you really struggle with the scale length of a standard 34-inch bass guitar then consider a short scale bass. They can be 30 or 32 inches and are much easier on the hands. They also sound remarkably deep and punchy, so you don't lose anything in terms of low end.

A 5-string bass has a wider neck than a 4-string, and 6-strings are wider still. Although you don't need huge hands to play these instruments, a good set up is going to be a big part of their playability.

A set up is where (amongst other things) the truss rod and bridge are tweaked to adjust the height of the strings above the frets. This is called the *action*, and a low one will make fretting much easier. Having the action too low, however, will compromise the tone, so find your preference (it's worth building a relationship with a good luthier or guitar technician who can help you).

Strings

Strings come in different *gauges*. Generally speaking, the thinner the gauge the easier it is to play. Bending strings is much easier with lighter strings. Different gauges, windings and materials also have different sounds.

Be aware of these different factors and get down to your local shop and try as many different combinations as you can. The bass you choose, and the strings and set up you use, will all be down to what tone you want to achieve and the way you want to play.

Amp

I'm a big advocate of doing what you can with the gear you have. Having a small practice amp at home is highly advisable as, without an amp, you may overcompensate to hear yourself and dig in a little too much. This will add strain to your hands and leave you overcompensating on a gig.

Once you have a bit of muscle memory and some good technique behind you, you *can* practice without an amp. It's certainly better than not playing at all because you don't have an amp or because of noise restrictions.

That said, great players don't make excuses. They put the hours in, do the right things and make the best of what they've got. This attitude will pay dividends in achieving your musical goals.

Next steps

I hope you've seen that there is often more than one way to play something on bass. The more options you have, the more expressive you can be. Techniques are just tools, and the more you have at your disposal, the more you'll be able to play what's in your head.

You will develop your own style based on your individual preferences. That's fine as long as you are playing with good technique, without strain or pain. If that's the case and you sound good, then it *is* good.

Technique is one piece in the puzzle of being a great bass player. It's an incredibly important, foundational piece, but remember that timing, taste, fretboard knowledge, applying theory, improvising, knowing lots of tunes, and developing good practice habits are also crucial.

Without a doubt, having excellent technique will make the whole learning process much more pleasurable as well as easier. I really hope you got a lot from this book. If you have any questions, I'd love to hear from you via **www.onlinebasscourses.com** or my social media channels.

If you found this book valuable, please consider leaving a nice review. This really helps and is always hugely appreciated.

Good luck and all the best!

Dan

Connect with Dan

Instagram: OnlineBassCourses

YouTube: OnlineBassCourses

Made in the USA
Las Vegas, NV
17 February 2022

44124549R00048